MORE PRAISE FOR *TURKEY:*
THE INSANE AND THE MELANCHOLY

"What a brave woman! And what a fine, stylish and intelligent writer! Mixing sarcasm, anger, wit, and irony as well as hard facts, Ece Temelkuran has provided us with an informative and moving account of Turkey's seemingly inexorable drift into authoritarianism."

Donald Sassoon, author of *The Culture of the Europeans*

"Part guide, part confidante, Ece Temelkuran brilliantly captures the neurosis at the heart of her country. An important book for anyone who wants to understand modern Turkey."

Padraig Reidy, editor of *Little Atoms*

ABOUT THE AUTHOR

Ece Temelkuran is one of Turkey's best-known authors and political commentators. She was previously a columnist for the *Milliyet* newspaper, before her outspoken criticism of government repression led to her losing her job. Her previous books in English include *Deep Mountain: Across the Turkish–Armenian Divide* (2010) and the poetry collection *Book of the Edge* (2010).

Ece has lived in Tunisia, Lebanon, Paris and Oxford to write her novels, which are published in several languages, and now divides her time between Istanbul and Zagreb.

TURKEY
THE INSANE AND THE MELANCHOLY

ECE TEMELKURAN
TRANSLATED BY ZEYNEP BELER

ZED
Zed Books
LONDON

Turkey: The Insane and the Melancholy was first published
in English in 2016 by Zed Books Ltd, The Foundry,
17 Oval Way, London SE11 5RR, UK.

www.zedbooks.net

Typeset in Haarlemmer by seagulls.net
Index by John Barker
Cover design by Clare Turner

A catalogue record for this book is available from the British Library.

ISBN 978-1-78360-890-4 hb
ISBN 978-1-78360-889-8 pb
ISBN 978-1-78360-892-8 pdf
ISBN 978-1-78360-891-1 epub
ISBN 978-1-78360-893-5 mobi

To the young people who died in the recent struggles,
whose coffins were heavier than their bodies.

CONTENTS

INTRODUCTION

YESTERDAY

"This is Turkey!"

This is quite possibly the most often used phrase in Turkey on any given day. It is used to allude to extraordinarily ludicrous situations and events. Always accompanied by a sardonic smile, in truth devoid of meaning, there is an agreement on a national level that the phrase can somehow account for anything. For instance, if an ambulance is late and then proceeds to run over the patient and kill him, you are allowed to say, in dramatic tones: "That's Turkey!"

You could plausibly laugh and say the same thing in the event that you observe a driver on the highway with his foot sticking out of the window – with no apparent casualties left in his wake: "That's Turkey!"

But wait! If you're kissing someone in plain sight in Istanbul and someone jabs you on the shoulder to shout the following, you have been warned:

"Whoa! This is Turkey! None of that here!"

You'd benefit from knowing that kissing is less seemly to the people of this country than fighting.

A sentence that begins with "This is" is quite crafty, simultaneously positing and dismissing shock. It both boasts

3

of a certain distinctiveness and explains away any lack of improvement as some kind of unalterable fate. It speaks of the melancholy of taking the great, long madness known as Turkey for what it is, of getting used to that madness, or, more accurately, resigning oneself to it. This phrase constitutes the core of the tragicomic nature of a country where every message has at least two meanings:

This is Turkey!

That is all fine and good, but what is "this" place?

Perhaps *this* isn't even a place. For, according to the definition taught since the country's founding, "this" is a *bridge*. "Between the East and the West" and "between Asia and Europe". Between the Orient and the Occident. This "in between-ness" has engendered hesitancy in the imaginations of nearly everyone who hails from here. As it is, from which side of the bridge does one best describe the bridge? According to the Republic founded in 1923, the answer is self-evident.

Every generation since the founding of the Republic of Turkey has studied the same map of the country at their desks in elementary school. According to this map, Turkey was the biggest country in the world and, naturally, in the very middle. It stood as a colossus in the midst of our founding father Atatürk's pledges: "Turk, be proud, work and trust!" and "Happy is the man who calls himself a Turk!" Europe hovered "above", full of colour. Inside the spectral countries were cities with pretty names and rivers of bright blue. Our forefathers praised this Eldorado as the ideal goal. "Below" was the East. The East was always grey-yellow in colour. Like the USSR,

4

it resembled a desert or a rough, hazy void. The cities were marked haphazardly. In this incarnation, the map said:

"Don't look down or to the right, look up. Above is a colourful and vivacious life. There is nothing below other than 'the dirty Arabs' and camels. There is nothing worthy of your curiosity. Get yourself out of there and run towards the West as fast as your feet can carry you."

On this map, the Republic thought it more fitting to define this country that bridged Asia and Europe, its government, and the children born here, by the west side of the bridge. It presented this "passage existence" as an identity to be proud of, not something to hesitate about – so much so that you would think we were all that was keeping the East and the West from being completely severed, and the whole world from simply falling apart. Thank heavens for Turkey! And it was our fate to swim towards the West in a perpetual state of passage.

However, those on the bridge had two big problems concerning who they were and what this place was. First of all, regardless of how breathlessly they swam towards the West, they kept being tugged backwards by the East side of the bridge. And that wasn't their only nightmare. Under the founding father's orders, they also had been given the mission of rising to the level of the people of the West and then surpassing that level. In his famous speech marking the tenth year of the Republic, Atatürk had ordained that we must "rise above the level of the conquering civilisations". This mission burdened people even more. They knew they were "below", but with the bravado of being on the same level as those "above", and they were simultaneously tugged backwards by the sense of insignificance pressuring them from the East side of their existence. They were pulled this way and that by an existential vacuum with dual suction: greatness and insignificance. It was as though Turkey had been cursed with the inability to find a mirror that would show it as it was, without overstating or understating.

And as if this weren't enough, another duality woven into the land's destiny served to doubly confuse the inhabitants of the bridge. On the tiny piece of land left over from the loss of an entire empire, even those who had thoroughly experienced the tragedy of war perceived the founding of Turkey to be a "great victory". The Ottoman had only been a burden anyhow! Young Turkey was ground zero, a new leaf. For a people who had lost everything to war, such motivation was naturally a necessity, but resetting history came at a cost. The "before" was abolished. We were grandchildren of a colossal empire, but that empire was worthless! Formal history invalidated the era of the empire, yet we all had to learn about the sultans and their times. The year 1923 constituted a milestone, but one with which we admittedly had an ambiguous association. "Before" was at once distasteful and a source of pride to us, a sovereignty we emulated even as we held it in contempt. The inhabitants of the bridge grew up with the befuddlement of children who witnessed history first-hand and then had to memorise a completely different version of events from the one they had witnessed. They became so accustomed to having everything labelled backwards that it no longer seemed strange that every sign had a double meaning. This is why the people of Turkey have never found the reaction "This is Turkey!" odd:

they are used to experiencing shock and indifference, laughter and tears. And they don't find it strange that they must both protest against and adapt to the situation, or that they have been forced to live with such complicated psyches.

* * *

So the years rolled on – decades, administrations and coups, massacres and football victories, hot and cold wars, riots and repressions, dreams dreamed and dreams wrecked for the love of the nation, and most of all the coffins, coffins, coffins. Each coffin was atoned for by planting another flag. The Koran, the Turkish flag and bread are all sacred in these lands. For generations, if any one of the three is found on the ground, it has to be kissed three times and placed on a high shelf. Soldiers, guerrillas, militants, journalists, writers, poets, labourers, students and children were killed, and after each killing it was loudly claimed, "No, they were not!"

"This" place preferred fury to grief. The speed with which funerals are carried out in Turkey might surprise a Westerner but really it shouldn't. For "This is Turkey!", and its bridge people, bent on survival, grew up being taught that grief is a waste of time.

Although those who wanted equality, justice and freedom for the nation were annihilated every time – either by a military regime or by the paramilitary forces of right-wing administrations – tables were set each night where people spoke of ways to save the country with more passion than they spoke of love. More shouting went on over the country than between two men in love with the same woman, more tears shed than by someone abandoned by a lover, more laughter emitted than by someone united with a loved one after many years of separation. The country always thrashed the children who loved it the most, and the people deigned to love those thrashed children only after their deaths. Around these same tables, people frequently wondered how it was that a country could be so cruel to its children.

There was an Ottoman tradition whereby sultans had their own brothers strangled to prevent claims to the throne, going as far as legalising fratricide. Could this have anything to do with the Prime Minister very comfortably telling a father who lost a son in the war in the south-east, "Military duty is no place to lie around, brother!"? Could the fact that this state was originally founded by children taken from their families and homelands have anything to do with the "state as father" complex that is revealed when Kurds, Alevis and Armenians are punished as though they have attacked a sacred father? Speculations abound, but one thing is evident: until the last decade, Turkey has been plagued by these very same maladies. And for the last decade, its tale has been one of attempting to cure those maladies with other, yet more complicated maladies ...

TODAY

"*You* are Turkey. Think big!"

Along with this slogan, countless gargantuan portraits of Recep Tayyip Erdoğan, possibly the most phenomenal character to grace Turkish political history, have been hanging all over Turkey in the past few years. Just like Atatürk's portrait before it, the image hovers together with the phrase: "Turk! Be proud, work, trust!" "This is Turkey!" no longer, however, but "the great Turkey!" By virtue of the rhetoric AKP has created with the help of its right-wing liberal intellectual following, "this is new Turkey", an "advanced democracy". As the party in power since 2002, AKP's political and social hegemony further serves to underscore its "sacred mission". To oppose the party is tantamount to opposing the concept of "the great Turkey", and, by proxy, threatening the "sacred mission". It means opposing Erdoğan, who is referred to as *reis* – "chief" – and is now striving to establish a presidential system from his chair as President at the AK Palace he has built. (Ironically, AK Palace means "White Palace", so is analogous to the White House.) Considering that, in this country, there are party members who openly claim that Erdoğan is the "chosen one" and that touching him is a form of worship, not to mention voters who clamour that they "wouldn't mind being the hair on his arse", this could be viewed as not only a political but a socio-psychological issue as well. Based on conservative and neoliberal values, the party's rhetoric isn't merely populist abracadabra working its magic on the undereducated masses. Up until now, since rising to power, AKP's spin doctors have been applauded in the most exceptional and esteemed circles of the West. Likewise, the mainstream media of the USA and Europe lauded AKP's rise to power with the declaration that "democracy has finally arrived in Turkey". AKP not only represented the perfect marriage between moderate Islam and democracy, but it was also a convincing model for the Arab world with its uncontrollable post-9/11 fury towards to West. When Turkey's secular intellectuals and writers tried to warn that such a "model" was not fit for the people of the Islamic world, let alone anywhere in the world, they were met with the ridicule of not only the neoliberals of Turkey but Western intellectuals as well. The critics were branded enemies of democracy, militants who wished to bring back the military whose clandestine authority over the government had been abolished by AKP. Also, because the economy was flourishing with money suddenly pouring into the country from some obscure source, intellectuals who were sceptical about AKP and its intentions for the system were further viewed and presented as archaic socialists or remnants of the Cold War. To be one of those intellectuals during AKP's first term in power meant permanent exile from respectable circles. For AKP was making some extraordinary promises. It spoke in sentences that libertarian movements had been soundlessly trying to form for quite a while. It spoke of non-Muslims and Kurds and individual freedoms. It condemned the military coup of 12 September 1980. It maintained that the army should be expelled from politics and railed at the top of its lungs for democracy. It pointed out that Turkey was one mosaic composed of a rich spectrum of ethnic and religious colours and gushed about the culture of coexistence. It was all so great and so wonderful! What was more, it brought a new definition to the bridge that was Turkey, and, through the "Middle Eastern initiative", reunited the nation with the lands it had turned its back on since the founding of the Republic. To a country that was jaded by its efforts to puff itself up and appear larger than it was in order to alleviate the sense of insignificance it felt in the presence of the West, AKP said: "Loosen up! After all, you're an elder brother to the Middle East even in your current state. And see, the West already sees us as a 'model country'!"

AKP was the symbol of the conservative capital that surfaced with the military coup of 1980, achieved leverage throughout Asia Minor, and gained its claws in the 1990s when it adopted the moniker "Anatolian Tigers". It wasn't for nothing that former President Abdullah Gül, cofounder of AKP, proclaimed: "We are the WASPs of this country." This political movement aimed to replace the older secular capital in the large cities and had been organising towards that aim for the past twenty years. AKP represented this class not only in terms of economic interest but also in lifestyle, world view, values and aesthetic. Under the new administration, the new bourgeoisie that hoped to replace the former secular bourgeoisie formed with the Republic's official support now had political representation and were "dedicated to national values". What those values were, AKP's newly founded provincialist culture would come to determine.

What endeared AKP to Turkey's masses was the promise that our relationship with the past would finally be mended. From the start, the party declared that we were the mighty grandchildren of the Ottoman and would once again assume our former grandiose, intimidating identity. However, it was also forced to invent a new Ottoman Empire that would be acceptable to the conservative masses. To this end, even the Prime Minister was wont to interrupt his duties to, say, comment on the women in the TV series *The Magnificent Century*, widely watched in the Balkans and Arabia as well as in Turkey, saying that they should dress more demurely, as well as claiming that Padishahs had been too busy riding their horses to have spent so much time with women. The following week's episode would see the women praying in the harem and a Suleiman the Magnificent who had wasted no time in clambering onto his horse, showing us what the reinvented Ottoman Empire was supposed to resemble. This was a minor example of the revision of culture; the Prime Minister did not stop there in his ambition to conservatise culture through the arts. He demolished the enormous peace statue erected in Kars and visible from Armenia because it didn't suit his tastes, and he also closely monitored the state theatre, ballet and opera. As an exemplary re-founding father, he shared his musical tastes with the masses. At rallies he would have the crowd repeat, as a pledge, the classical Turkish song "We walked down this path together":

"We walked down this path together / together we got wet in the pouring rain / Now everything in all the songs / reminds me of you."

Over the years, we collectively witnessed a love song become the marching tune for AKP's sacred mission.

At times, the Prime Minister's relatives dealt with cultural issues he couldn't find time to get involved in. When his daughter was needled for chewing gum at an interactive play, as the script required, it resulted in the actor in question being investigated and receiving a pay cut.

* * *

Neither the West nor the majority of Turkey's intelligentsia paid any attention to the criticism expressed during that time. Yes, the army was finally being exiled from politics; however, this was being done through huge political trials that infringed the law. What was more, with each trial a few more journalists or politicians were convicted and proclaimed to be members of clandestine coup-perpetrating organisations that might or might not exist. There were also intellectuals who believed that the infringement of the law was a small price to pay if it meant the army would be barred from politics and openly said so.

Those who applauded as AKP deemed the social democrats "supporters of the state founding party CHP", conservative parties other than themselves "old-fashioned", and socialists "anarchists", as in the coup of 1980, by extension declaring themselves to be the only real democratic movement in the country, were soon once again witnessing unions, associations and political parties being straightened out through extrajudicial means. As a political and social movement made tangible in the form of Erdoğan, AKP continued to make lovely promises. It "initiated" and obliterated Turkey's political taboos. The Kurdish initiative, the Alevi initiative, the intellectual initiative, the Romanian initiative … by receiving long-ignored groups at his breakfast table at the Dolmabahçe Palace, Erdoğan allowed them to be recognised officially. This seemingly democratic gesture, however, did not include dissidents. The government's "initiatives" were made in cooperation with the Alevis it favoured, the Kurds it picked, and the Romanians who supported AKP. Turkey "as you like it" was invited to breakfast and the rest waited to be branded as terrorists, which they were bound to be sooner or later.

Yes, the Kurdish initiative was happening, the administration gearing up for negotiations with the PKK, although at the same time it was silencing the press to avoid answering questions about the Kurds who were taken for terrorists and shot on the Iraqi border, as well as having journalists such as myself fired through phone calls to media executives when they continued to write about the issue. In the meantime, the "peace proceedings" between the PKK and Turkey progressed, but were kept hidden from the public and anyone who might voice an opinion. Prime Minister Erdoğan's word was sufficient, after all, and this was just how things were done now. Workers' rights, children's rights, women's rights, personal liberties ... all were guaranteed by the Prime Minister placing a hand on his chest and saying, "I promise." The enthusiasm many a dissident intellectual displayed in believing the words of their assumed re-founding father was painful to witness. And the bitterest part of it was when, in the midst of all the promises of minority rights and democratisation, state officials who plainly protected the slain Armenian journalist Hrant Dink's murderers were cleared by the AKP administration and some Armenian intellectuals were able to find it in themselves to defend this.

* * *

At any rate, political mechanisms were increasingly losing importance as the "balcony speeches" given by Erdoğan at AKP headquarters entered politics as a legitimate institution. Even those who sensed the dangers of recent developments found solace in the honeyed words of Erdoğan. So much so that Erdoğan's claim that "Those who don't vote for us are also part of this nation's colour palette," made during the infamous balcony speech of AKP's second term in power, was taken as a sign of "advanced democracy", and his "forgiveness" and "tolerance" for the dissidents met with applause. The article I wrote at the time – "We have been reduced to the country's side dish" – garnered hate mail and sardonic accusations of paranoia, which I now recall with a bitter smile.

What both its fans in the international sphere and the "aligned" intellectuals of Turkey refused to comprehend from 2002 up until about the middle of AKP's second term in power was that not only was the country being conservatised, but the gradual aggravation of anti-terror laws were aimed at creating an obedient society. Through changes to the Constitution, AKP had also gained control of the implementation of law, thus completely demolishing all stabilising mechanisms, political or judicial. Not to mention certain freedoms becoming unavailable in spite of the law, due to the social phenomenon known as "community pressure", and conservative values increasingly constricting secular lifestyles in ways as difficult to prove as they were tangible. No one may have been telling young women in Anatolia to cover their heads, but it was touted as exemplary and those who didn't conform were treated as though they were walking around nude. Surveys showed that AKP put the screws on economics as well as on day-to-day life, and employers that refrained from expressing loyalty to the party were immobilised. The party's ambitions for influence went as far as accusing the Constitutional Court of "political bias" whenever they ruled against

AKP's interests. The nation had entered, in every sense, a top-speed process of "Dubaisation". Although the term falls decidedly short, if I had to sum up Turkey's present situation in one word, this would be it:

Dubaisation!

In this book, you will be able to read in great detail about what that means.

In 2013, however, when the mainstream media in the West was at a loss for words to describe the madness that started in Taksim Gezi Park and proceeded to spread all over the country in the form of protests, this was due to the Western media's severe misreading of the story's beginning. To understand the Turkey that had risen up with Gezi, journalists had to go back and retell the story they had been telling for the last eleven years, but this time with the facts. Not feeling up to the task, some international media outlets persisted in viewing the uprising as the "clash of the obstinate seculars with the conservative society", despite the dozens of Islamists and conservative organisations that had taken part in the protests, refusing to see that it was the last chance for the ignored and oppressed factions to make their voices heard. In the eyes of Prime Minister Erdoğan and followers of AKP, the uprising was the doing of "outside forces, traitors, those who would see Turkey's progress impeded". Many felt that the more the Prime Minister spoke, the closer his rhetoric resembled that of the coup-perpetrating generals he had claimed to oppose in order to come to power. Meanwhile, the media system established by AKP increasingly made targets of journalists who reported on the uprising and writers, artists and businessmen who supported it, purporting them to be "provocateurs" and printing full-page portraits, while pro-AKP columnists "called out to public prosecutors" to immediately prosecute these people.

In the period after the Gezi riots, shortly after proclaiming his disinclination to be impartial, Recep Tayyip Erdoğan was elected President. Now he resides in a gargantuan, 1,100-roomed palace he had built in Ankara in the Atatürk Forest Farm, a symbol of the Republic, uprooting the trees there. Not only did no comprehensive political organisation emerge from the Gezi riots, there is also no political formation at parliamentary level that is up to the task of presenting a viable alternative to AKP. Everyone, from the richest to the poorest, knows their fate depends on what comes out of the Chief's mouth, while he poses on the staircase of his palace next to the mannequins representing the previous sixteen Turkish state leaders. Although the majority of social media users took this for a Photoshopped joke, we need to keep reminding ourselves, day by day, that what we are living is no joke but reality. AKP's spokesmen ceaselessly remind us that those dissatisfied with the state of things should leave the country or learn to live with it. With the current situation in Turkey, the question of the future leaves the masses either too jaded to answer or too angry to speak. AKP and the President, however, have a very clear answer. All the party slogans say the same thing:

"Objective 2023!"

Meaning they plan to stick around for at least another decade.

TOMORROW

"What will become of this nation of ours!"

Foreigners are likely to think the exclamation mark quaint; in Turkey, however, this isn't a question. Although it appears to be one, it tends to be enunciated with a troubled exclamation at the end. The sentence communicates a deep sense of frustration. While directly translatable, it is entirely too Turkish for its sentiment to be transposed into another language. "What is to become of this nation of ours" states that things are bad and will get worse still. Its head between its hands, the sentence mopes in a state of desperation. In desperation, it implores the interlocutor for a remedy to this worrisome course of events. It asks, "Is there any hope?", and sometimes even goes as far as to say, "It looks like there really isn't anything more to do." Whereas the administration's sentence regarding the future – "Objective 2023!" – is ambitious and clear, the corresponding slogan of the masses is this:

"What will become of this nation of ours!"

Because they don't see Turkey's future through the government's lens: that is, out of the windows of the newly built high rises and shopping malls. What they do see instead is this:

- With the 1,400 per cent increase in killings of women in the last seven years, a country that has practically declared a war on women.
- The 180-odd people killed by police bullets in the last eight years of AKP's administration, most of them young

and some of them children, and the officers who went unpunished.

- The hundreds of prisoners and detainees of political trials convicted through false evidence and the courtrooms erected within (!) the new concentration camp-like prisons for these trials.
- The pro-regime crowds that support the "enemy criminal law" implemented by the administration against dissidents, believing that those who go against the police must die, even if they are children.
- A docile army of indigents who, in their awe of power, believe it fair and right that a single man should have absolute unsupervised authority – and live in an enormous palace as well.
- The administration's blatant protection of the Prime Minister's adviser, who, after a disaster resulting in the deaths of 301 miners, kicked the miners protesting for their rights, or the numerous ministers whose certified malpractices have been exposed.
- The hundreds of journalists sacked through calls to media executives because they presumed to write about the above or, for instance, the fact that radical Islamist militants were being taken into the country over the Syrian border.
- Members of the opposition being put in hospital by members of the party in power in the Grand National Assembly, after which event the injured members were photographed by said members of the party in power and the images posted on social media for ridicule.

- Worker's organisations, professional associations and universities razed by political trials before being reconfigured on the premise of ignorance and subordination to the government.
- Children powerless in the face of an education system made increasingly more reactionary and totalitarian by way of mandatory classes in religion and Ottoman Turkish.
- And the creeping sense of being on the verge of losing our wits after listening to the hundreds of supporters who are all over our screens with assurances that all this paints a picture of "the great Turkey" and "advanced democracy" …

What you won't learn from the statistics or the political analyses of international experts, however, is this extremely important fact:

In the past five years, the most commonly spoken words in mainly private conversations and homes across Turkey are the following:

- "I can't handle all that's happening anymore. I don't want to hear it."
- "This country has truly gone insane. It's gone stark raving mad."
- "I don't watch the news anymore because it's just too much."
- "It's all so weird I feel like it's going on in some other country."

- "Is this really happening, or are we in some collective nightmare?"
- "It's like someone is pulling a huge *Candid Camera* on Turkey."

This is because a society overwhelmed by the administration's judicial obstruction of political representation, the impairment of legal routes through the factionalisation of the entire institution of law, the unmitigated silencing of the press and the "illegitimation" of the streets through anti-terror laws is force-fed declarations of how well the country is being run, every day, on TV. We are like children who receive a thrashing every day only to be told it never happened. More than anything else, our most deeply felt condition is this:

"We are being driven mad!"

And that, if this administration's objective is truly 2023, "the administration in this country wants no one but its own!"

Of late, the most commonly shared quote on social media is one of Tezer Özlü's from the era of the military coup:

"This country does not belong to us but to those who would like to kill us."

Told that Turkey is heading towards fascism, the European reader may think, based on her own historical experience, that this is not unlike a teenager howling "This is fascism!" when he is told to clean up the mess in his room. And it is indeed up for debate whether what Turkey is approaching could be called fascism. But the truth is that today even ordinary people in Turkey share on their Facebook profiles the famous statement by the priest Martin Niemöller: "First they came for socialists and I did not speak up because I was not a Socialist... and there was no one left to speak for me." "When is it my turn?," people are thinking. For – although the reasons may never be set out in official history – even the most politically uninvolved storekeepers and grocers of Turkey believe the government is tapping their phones.

Who, then, will determine Turkey's future? The masses looking out at Turkey through the "Objective 2023!" lens, or those who wake every morning to the sensation of asphyxiation and losing their mind?

Those in Turkey who live amidst feelings of asphyxiation and losing their wits revolted in the summer of 2013. It all started when three trees in the Taksim Square in the centre of Istanbul were uprooted for highway construction. For weeks, the entire country, with the exception of two cities, were on the streets day and night to protest on behalf of society's other half and its distress and sense of being driven mad, as well as the administration's irrational, fallacious, unlawful and unscrupulous methods. After Tahrir Square and Madrid, and exactly like the crowds in those places, people protested with laughter, even though they were risking death. Eleven died and more than 8,000 were injured during the Gezi riots. None of the perpetrators of violence against the people were prosecuted, but close to 6,000 protestors were put on trial. Yet three years later *the ghost of Gezi still continues to haunt Turkey.*

Today, an unsettled sense of discord still presides over not only Turkey but also Egypt, Spain, Greece and many other countries in the world. Stripped of all of its words and rhetoric during the transition from the Cold War to the unipolar world order, unrest increasingly takes the form of pure fury on all the impoverished streets of the world. Perhaps, very soon, Tahrir, Gezi or Madrid will see the beginnings of a new "wordless revolt" that has nothing to say, not one word, sentence or demand. Or …

Or *Andalusia Reloaded*! There's no other solution but to return the words and the knowledge of being an able mass to the poor, the repressed and the wronged, not only of Turkey but of all other lands. This is why all revolts, both above and below the navel of the Earth, must be "united". The East and the West must be reconstructed at the point of contact: that is, Andalusia. In the succeeding pages you will also be able to find a few words on Andalusia Reloaded.

Tomorrow … it seems to contain Eldorado no matter the language in which it is uttered. Today, however, when one says it in Turkish, an ominous tone creeps into one's voice, just like when one says the words "This is Turkey!"

A word before we begin: When talking to a foreigner about one's own troubled, ill-fated and perplexing country, one tends to feel ethically disinclined – as one should: to avoid betraying not just one's country but also the truth and the integrity of truth, to avoid offence. I feel anxious that the things I am about to disclose will paint a picture of Turkey as one enormous pathology. It isn't. This quaint country has a constitution of its own. Although I will be describing the fouler aspects of this constitution, I would like to reject the assumption that this constitutes its entirety… to describe a house "from the outside" should not be a privilege exclusive to those who are not in it.

YESTERDAY

"Geography means destiny." – **Ibn Khaldun**

"I am unsure as to how one goes about expressing a point of view completely at odds with the Western world. It is in a sense an irrational – unwesternly – point of view. A point of view with an unintended touch of comedy, a view that to me is rather naive. It is my impression that we are a rather immature people who are drastically inclined to interpret events and reality on the basis of miracle and myth. In ways that would make a rational Westerner chuckle when to us it is deadly serious." – **Oğuz Atay, Diaries**

"Yesterday is yesterday, today is today, and tomorrow is tomorrow!"

Uttered in English by a guest speaker from Turkey, this bizarre exclamation naturally might have taken by surprise the audience gathered at Cornell University on 7 October 2003. The bald and overweight elderly man at the lectern beamed as he translated, word by word, the axiomatic quote whose Turkish original he had made a custom of repeating through the years. After all, voicing this profound insight had earned him a decade in total governing his country as Prime Minister, between 1965 and 1993, before a stint as President, as well as the moniker "Father", which was to endure until his death. The man at the lectern was Süleyman Demirel, Turkey's ninth President, and he was completely assured that the tautology, even more glaring in its ludicrousness when recited at Cornell University, was even now a perfect analogy for Turkey's relationship to its past:

"Yesterday is yesterday, today is today."

In Turkey, this widespread aphorism is used not only by politicians but also by ordinary people on a daily basis. Ask anyone, "How can you say such-and-such when you were claiming the exact opposite yesterday?" and they will respond, with just as much aplomb and glee as Demirel himself:

"Yesterday is yesterday ..."

If it's consistence you're after or you mean to question morality, you had better forget it. For whatever was said or done yesterday was yesterday. The aplomb and glee stem from the comfort of this legitimised point of view. No one can judge you based on your past deeds, just as the state cannot be held responsible today for what it did yesterday. Those who attempt to question the past are destined to be forgotten, just like everything else that belongs in the past. The issue at hand is not yesterday but the present, or, even more importantly, the future. The aphorism is also relevant to political ethics. In that sense, Turkish politicians are the most privileged politicians on the planet. For Turkey is one of those exceptional countries where, when a politician is questioned about a past deed, the inquiring party is the one who is insulted and told off. To question the past signals inadequacy, naivety, obsolescence, an inability to deal with the present, and being a spoilsport, for which you will ultimately be dropped from the game. To question the past means early defeat. You have failed in catching up with the present and being up to date. Better to take a new position in step with the changing times.

* * *

Better to forget. And, even better, to forget – or remember – whenever and however it is deemed suitable by the current political climate. That is why, for Turkey, the past is a constantly shifting, ever-changing point in the distance. The Gallipoli Victory, with Mustafa Kemal Atatürk amongst its commanders, is painfully and ecstatically recent. But that same 1915 can sometimes feel like *a million years ago* ...

* * *

The roots of this common moral stance reach way back, to a *practice of forgetting* starting on a day in the far past. It is thanks to this practice that the torture of hundreds of thousands of people during the military coup of 1980, the incomprehensible atrocities inflicted on the Kurds in the Diyarbakır Prison or – just a month ago – a mine tragedy that took 301 lives, or – just two weeks ago – a child killed by a police bullet or – just three days ago – thousands of olive trees unlawfully cut down, or the fact that those who called for peace with the Kurds last year are rallying for war today, or – just this morning – the rape and slaughter of an adolescent girl can all be considered to have happened a long, long time ago. It's so long ago ... *it's practically prehistoric.*

THE ORIGINS OF FORGETTING

"What, those? They're *practically prehistoric* ..."

If you ask the local villagers and townspeople about the old Armenian churches, left derelict in the centre or at the edges of cities or in the midst of what are now the fields and hillsides of Anatolia, they are bound to say to you: "What, those? They're *practically prehistoric.*"

"Just what do you mean, prehistoric? It's barely been a hundred years. The Armenians were driven out and massacred in 1915. What do you mean *prehistoric*?!"

Let's say you dared venture the hatred this reply is likely to provoke. He shakes his head indifferently, and might say, "Oh sure, the Armenians. They left."

Where did they go?

"It was a long time ago. They left by way of that bridge."

So where did they go?

"Left by way of that bridge, over there."

You needn't ask, "Then after the bridge, where?" for the answer is evident. Packing up (or without packing up), one day, for reasons unknown, the Armenians set out by the hundreds of thousands for "prehistoric" times.

In Fethiye, well known to European and Russian tourists, there are vacant stone houses sitting atop a hill. They stand there without windows or doorframes, resembling corpses with gouged-out eyes and gaping mouths. Like ghosts frozen mid-scream. When you try to trace Kayaköy's history, the story begins sometime BC and invariably ends up at "practically prehistoric". Once again, the Rum population who resided here just left by the thousands one day for reasons unknown. No one has taken up residence in the village since. It just sits there like some cursed hilltop town from a fairy tale. Just ask the villagers and they'll point you towards the bridge over which the Rums left. They'll tell a story, the missing pieces of which fall from sight, one by one, from whichever bridge was en route to the *practically prehistoric*.

The oldest bathhouse in Ankara is called the Şengül *Hammam*. If you ask for directions, you'll come up with a newly named avenue or street that no one really knows. Only if you persist will they tell you its actual location, the one mired in their collective memory: "In the old Jewish Town."

There are no longer any Jews in the Jewish Town. So where are the Jews? Or the Christians of Ankara, for that matter? There will doubtless be a bridge at a convenient distance for them to gesture towards. It is there for the Assyrians of Mardin and the Rums of Trabzon. For the thousands of Alevi Kurds of Dersim. Since the founding of the Republic, the bridges have been funnelling all its narratives into an endless void, a black hole in the shape of its "befores" and "yesterdays". Ironically, most of Turkey's bridges are named after either Atatürk or the Republic …

* * *

The transformation of historical truths into fragmented stories or even, increasingly, fairy tales, the amnesia that provides politicians with the facility to laughingly claim that "Yesterday is yesterday, today is today," could be claimed to be a state policy – or even that the country has been founded on this very same amnesia. The Republic of Turkey has depended on forgetfulness; it's true. The founders of this country proclaimed the Republic to be year zero, thus rendering prehistoric anything that had happened before. As such, those who "left" (were driven out, annihilated, compelled to leave) passed over a bridge into prehistory and now speaking about them is prohibited. The reason for the silence, however, isn't any official prohibition, but rather an agreed-upon forgetting that has gradually come to encompass everyone, citizen by citizen. It isn't as if this practice of forgetting has been forced on us by the state at gunpoint. In the words of the essayist Nurdan Gürbilek, who dwells on and writes about Turkey's "spirit":

"The Turkish state of mind or the original Turkish spirit is just as closely associated with the acute desire for immidiate change of place as it is with its persistent inability to reach that goal."

In this sense, time, for this nation, is also merely something to be trodden on while passing through. To live here means to strive for immediate arrival in the future. For the future-bound, those who recall the past are the rickety pieces of junk they zoom past in their ultramodern cars. Those who remember have something of the old, useless, broken and debased about them. It must be due to this that the mothers of the disappeared, who have been meeting on Istiklal Avenue every Saturday for many years, are viewed less like their revered contemporaries in Argentina and more as an "old-fashioned" spectacle. We don't have an inkling about how many hundreds of weeks they have waited here, the mothers we have watched get old while the photos of the lost children they hold in their laps remain forever young. This lack of curiosity, this ready listlessness and indifference is learned. Just like forgetting was learned in 1915, so too is the reluctance for recollection and the dismissal of curiosity. These women don't intrigue us, in the same way that we don't wonder why the old Armenian buildings in the centre of Istanbul are vacant – if we see them at all, that is. On the hyper-touristy Istiklal Avenue, along which flows the entire world, the Saturday Mothers whose children were lost in the unsolved murders of the 1990s now seem to be merely a static monument of shame for the Japanese tourists who stop and soberly snap pictures. The inability to see even when history sits up and bites us can only be due to a well-practised blindness. Today, Turkey has become a true master of the forgetfulness that it has perfected through repetition of the practice of forgetting, disinterest and blindness that started in the wake of the country's founding. Everyone on the streets is wont to tell you the same: "Turkey has the memory of a goldfish!"

Oddly, when this is said, the luxuriating grin often accompanying the "Yesterday is yesterday, today is today" statement is nowhere to be seen. Yet, as also mentioned at the beginning of this book, being compelled to experience two different emotions by one situation, to read two contradictory meanings into one sign, is part of this country's temperament. After all, "This is Turkey!"

HOW IS INDIFFERENCE LEARNED?

This is how.

Every child who grew up on the West coast like me will remember those nights. The International Fair has opened. In essence a commercial and cultural fair, for Izmir's residents it's more like a traditional week of amusement. Families go on day and night trips. They browse the pavilions allocated to country representatives in the forested park grounds in the middle of the city. For the children, however, the greatest pleasure is found in the flashing lights of Lunapark. Starting during the day and extending into Lunapark at night, the merriment soon draws to a close and it is time to return home, with all the children exhausted. And if you happen to be past the age when you can be picked up and carried, you whine fruitlessly: "But I'm so tired, mum!"

Strangely, anyone who has ever grown up in Izmir has received the same reply to their whining:

"It's because of the electric cables passing underneath here. That's why the fair makes people so tired."

You grow up hearing this and are always just as exhausted with every fair season. Having grown up to adulthood with this explanation, those children are bound to tell their own children the same thing:

"It's because of the electric cables passing underneath here ..."

To begin to understand that the tension below ground stems from something other than electric cables, that we are exhausted not by "currents" below the fair but by the ghosts lurking below the surface of our memories – that requires a lot of growing up.

* * *

It had never occurred to me to wonder about this enormous blank space in the middle of the city of Izmir where the Izmir International Fair was situated. This was despite the fact that I had already written the book *Deep Mountain: Across the Turkish–Armenian Divide* and that I was aware that this state of indifference in Turkey was conditioned or learned behaviour. And yet each "Turkish" child is unknowingly instructed in not asking or not thinking to ask why the owners of those beautiful old apartments left and when, or how it was that the congregations of the magnificent churches in Anatolia suddenly vanished, or why those who were once here no longer are. Despite knowing all this, for years the fair continued to exist in my mind as a place that was "exhausting due to electric cables". I never wondered how there could be such an empty stretch right in the middle of the city. It never even occurred to me to take this as a sign that there was something there to wonder about. No matter how ludicrous, first impressions are resistant to correction. Learned forgetfulness and indifference aren't things that can be cured so easily, even by the most willing. So, finding out that the enormous expanse in the middle of Izmir had once been the Armenian and Rum district, that it had been burned to the ground … eradicating one's learned blindness could be a greater challenge than one could ever bargain for.

Lying is exhausting. With each telling the lie deepens, grows, becomes more complicated. After a while, the body of the lie surpasses the truth you have been trying to hide. The roots of the lie increasingly draw nourishment from your soul. The lie exhausts you; it eats away at you. That is why a motherland that, since its creation, has practised relating a history of victories rather than defeats, of festivities instead of massacres, of rebirth in paradise instead of death, exhausts us and eats away at us.

This must be why the people you address – the villager asked about the Armenian church, the townsman who has no idea where Kayaköy's residents went, the urbanite in Ankara who acts like she doesn't know about the history of the bathhouse – are wont to tell you something different once the conversation intensifies. The villager, for instance, might tell you that he learned cooking, weaving and bricklaying from Armenians. Or, overcome with the sadness of a calamity she herself never witnessed, a resident of Izmir might raise her *rakı* glass to old friends, in the direction of the visible lights of the Greek islands. Or a resident of Ankara might recall what the Jews used to do on Mondays, how he used to covet their festivities. They were never mourned because they were supposedly forgotten. And those who remain here have stories of their own. Each family tells of a journey that starts with a faraway tale. "My kin came from far, far away …" – that's the first sentence in the stories of many families in Turkey. Much was lost on that journey and many hardships encountered before settling here. Such is the bloody and woeful story concealed beneath the oft-repeated cliché of Anatolia's "bridge of passage". Now even those who have remained here bear the anxiety of the bridge they are in the process of crossing.

* * *

One justification for Turkey's memory loss, related as it is to the past but not limited to the past, as well as eclipsing the present day, is that: "There is just too much going on in the country right now – it's impossible to keep track of it all." It's true: much does go on. There can be enough items on the agenda for Turkey in one day to last a European country an entire year. Considering the state of the political and social agenda, it's like we are all extras in a Jackie Chan film. We are dealt slaps and kicks at such a fast pace we cannot count them. We barely get a chance to cope with one blow before we receive another. Part of the reason, however, is that we never could, or did, pause the film and question the first blow that was dealt.

* * *

The expunging of the events of 1915 from Turkey's official history established a practice of forgetting. The rest is just a prolonged and uninterrupted loop. As such, Demirel's aphorism – "Yesterday is yesterday, today is today" – is not his personal invention but rather an apt evaluation of Turkey's essence. After all, Demirel was so perceptive about his people, who embraced him with cries of "Father! Father!" at rallies, he stopped at nothing to have three left-wing youths hanged in 1971 to make an example of them. As the executions were being voted on in Parliament, he turned to face the members of his own right-wing party and bellowed, "Raise your hands! Raise them!" The executions of the three young men were to go down in Turkey's political history as the murder of innocence, and striving so hard to make it happen was only possible with the assurance that those days would be forgotten. (The young men – Deniz Gezmiş, Hüseyin Inan and Yusuf Aslan – are leading symbols of Turkey's culture of dissidence. Keep reading and you'll find out about their resurrection decades later.) Ultimately, both Demirel and the people know that fathers are capable of killing and then declaring the past null and void. That we should forget; that we should not speak of it. That, in the end, all those who leave use the bridge that erases memory …

We could be considered as children who have been forced to turn a blind eye to the murder committed by their father. Since the very beginning, that is.

The subject of fatherhood is worth consideration. Let us stay with it a while.

ORPHANS, FATHERS AND RESENTMENT

All I know is that there's a curse on this country. We're being made to pay for something, some original sin. I look back at our history. There was the coup in 1971, when they hanged so many of our kids. But it wasn't the first time. So I go back further, to the 1930s, when the seeds of modern Turkey were sown and so many people were executed. That wasn't when it started either. Perhaps, I say to myself, it started when the Ottomans moved out of tents and into palaces. You know, when the early Ottomans first began seizing young boys in Balkan villages to put them into the service of the Sultan. It was some of those orphaned boys who rose to positions of power and ran the state. Perhaps those boys' mothers cursed us way back then. Or could it be that …*

In my most recent novel, *Time of the Mute Swans*, which takes place in the summer of 1980, Aydın (a state official in his thirties, semi-intellectual) comes to the above conclusion a few months prior to the last military coup. He wonders about the earliest origins of the merciless, vulgar, atrocious, oppressive and exhausting system of this country that consumes even the dissidents. He wonders: "Why doesn't this country

---

* Translated by Kenneth Dakan.

love its children?" And he arrives at the conclusion that the state tradition is built on the resentment of those orphaned children. He feels that its soil is cursed. I can't say if he is right or not. It is, after all, not a very scientific conclusion. But, at the very least, this singular observation is bound to be shared by most.

If you were to scan the archives of all the newspapers published during Turkey's history, you would see this: all politicians – be they party leaders or parliamentary candidates – incessantly and expressly speak of "orphans' rights". Melodramatic at best, this rhetoric is part of most electoral speeches. So much so that you would think that orphans made up the majority of voters in Turkey's parliamentary elections. Candidates, by this reasoning, are not politicians but fathers vying for the approval of orphans. It seems that my epigraph from one of Turkey's most significant writers, Oğuz Atay, is true, but perhaps it lacks something. Not only are we a nation of children but, simultaneously, we are also a country that feels orphaned, or is taught to feel as such, or is easily able to feel as such. "A father both loves and punishes," us orphans have been taught to think. That we perceive a blow to be a caress is because it is the only kind of touch we have ever felt.

Have you ever seen an unloved child? The children in the orphanage? They cling to the first person who gives them any attention. Just like a cat weaned too early will suckle on its owner's hands, they latch on and will not let go. Initially, this gives rise to a joyful, bittersweet pang. Then a strange kind of anxiety takes over:

"What if she never lets go?"

41

Ultimately, you just want to cut loose. You feel that being an object of desire will overwhelm you. It's a weird kind of uneasiness. Never having had anyone, never having been loved by anyone, could make one desirous of a father to cling to and become one with. No matter what the cost …

For Westerners, the word "father" is likely to evoke primarily Our Holy Father, a priest at a church, or perhaps even a Mafia leader. For Turkey, however, it has more of a corporeal presence. The speaker at the lectern ought not to talk about economic figures, to display any kind of consistency regarding the past, or to present a rational argument. Let him be as Middle Eastern a father figure as possible and the votes are his.

It seems that this is the general state of things in Turkey. Like an orphan scurrying about for his father and, once he finds him, clinging to his leg, ready to go wherever he is told to go. In that sense, this is a region of the world where those reticent about the longing of orphans, or the insatiability of that longing, would not have much luck in politics. This is a political universe where self-appointed "orphan fathers" have the most luck, presume to strive for leadership and are guaranteed centre stage. Orphan fathers who have the stomach to beat recognition into their orphans …

"SUCH A GENERATION WE SHALL RAISE …"

"Such a generation we shall raise after you that they will not remember you."

There is this grandfather who nowadays lives in a cute little house in a coastal town. He paints in oils. He has no talent but plenty of determination, getting better at it every day. Though not exactly endearing, he seems harmless enough. The quote above belongs to this very charming grandad:

"Such a generation we shall raise that they will not remember you."

"Grandpa coup" addressed these words to the left-wing, progressive, democrat and organised people he had imprisoned, murdered and tortured in the military coup of 1980. In those days he used to paint in blood rather than oils. And "grandpa coup" was just as incompetent at painting back then as he is today – although he was equally determined. The canvas of Turkey painted during his leadership in 1980 looked like this:

- People's cultural centres shut down, with official religious schools opening up in their place.
- Philosophy classes were abolished in favour of compulsory religion classes, and talk of politics was banned in universities.
- There were as many prisons erected as there were unions and professional associations he had shut down.
- Multinational banks agreed to be built in place of the unions he had ploughed over.
- Teachers and students were manufactured and programmed to say "Yes, commander!" in place of all the teachers and commanders he had convicted.

Thousands were killed or went missing in dubious circumstances, tens of thousands tortured, exiled or denationalised.

The canvas this agreeable grandfather painted in blood and fear was at least as dead as the still lives he would paint years later in his retirement.

Just like Demirel, the coup's general Kenan Evren became a father figure to those who confused violence with love; similarly, he thoroughly enjoyed the luxuries of the "yesterday is yesterday" mentality, and died quietly while this book was being prepared for print. Even our culture, which prefers us to speak favourably of the dead, didn't stop us from speaking less than favourably once he had gone. In the papers and on TV, the news of his death was practically ignored.

The part of my story that concerns this old man centres on a true incident of forgetting or forced forgetfulness. Although only thirty-five years have passed since the bloody military coup he perpetrated, today even thirty-somethings – unless they are particularly invested in political history – think of him as an art-loving, affable grandad.

* * *

Joyful harbinger of a "generation without ideology", or sometimes "a generation that won't remember", Kenan Evren was the general of the military coup that took place on 12 September 1980. Today, Evren is remembered, along with the four other generals who were responsible for the coup, in two respects: either as the elderly painting aficionado who ended the "sibling quarrel" between 1971 and 1980, or as the cruel general who created his own brand of fascism through his annihilation of Turkey's democracy. The misconception shared by both of these incomplete recollections is that one person changed history in one day. Whereas, as you know, fascism isn't when bad guys suddenly materialise and kick the living daylights out of the good guys. Fascism is the gradual loss of humanity. The progression is so slow and slight as to be invisible to the naked eye.

Of all disasters, fascism is the most adept shape-shifter. Although the appearance and character of this old acquaintance have been described to us thousands of times over, whenever it approaches we fail to recognise it at sufficient distance. By the time it draws near and introduces itself, it's too late. For it harbours a secret that corrupts everything it touches. Not kills, corrupts … like mildew and humidity.

Fascism spreads out over time. It does this by creating a hesitation reminiscent of hypothermia-induced sleep. Phrases such as "Could it be?", "Let's just wait it out", "Maybe it won't be as bad as we think" slowly numb us. It is the greatest illusionist of our times. It has the ability to make the bad look like the good. At certain points in history, this ability combines with a veneer that makes invisible the unbearably awful elements of its constitution. Although justice is invariably sought, and a few scapegoats rounded up after enough time has passed, the malevolent ghost of fascism is never completely banished from our planet.

Fascism doesn't kill people from the outset; it transforms them. Its victory is in its facility to change what people are made of. Respect for one's fellow man is the first thing to go. The game begins when the process of legitimisation that engenders compliance and renders cruelty acceptable is initiated in the minds of the majority. For compliance, the nation's people must already be on the road to madness. World history has shown us that when the character of humanity is in enough disarray, entire societies can fall ill and take to their beds, never to get up again.

Each murder, massacre and act of cruelty in the history of a nation that isn't accounted for injects venomous blood, drop by drop, into a people's veins. And when all the blood in their veins has been replaced – a bit of blood, a bit of flour, a bit of blood, a bit of flour – the new citizens will be ready to applaud as a statue of tyranny is erected before their very eyes. The character of this new citizen isn't described very favourably in the ensuing pages of history. But once you change the character, it is easy to change the rest …

And that's how it happened in Turkey. The 1971 coup, which preceded the one in 1980, started to inject the mildew and corruption of fascism into the country's veins. What with the crisis of representation in politics, the street skirmishes that couldn't or wouldn't be contained and the economic crisis, by the time 12 September 1980 arrived the majority was ready to applaud the coup – or, at best, stay silent.

As it is, fascism wasn't imposed on the country's governance in one day by one general or by a group of generals. It is extremely difficult to explain the issue to European readers. I can practically picture the expression that is likely to appear on readers' faces as they read about Turkey's relationship with fascism, no matter what bloody examples I can think of to give them.

"Don't make a mountain out of a molehill!" they'll say.

We don't refer to the events of 1971 as a coup, unlike those of 1980, as they were not exactly that. Let's call it the military's sleight-of-hand adjustment of the political equilibrium: on 12 March 1971, Süleyman Demirel's administration was brought down by a memorandum signed by four generals of the highest military rank and read out on the state channel's news broadcasts.

Parliament wasn't closed, political parties weren't barred from activity, and no administrators were arrested. The administration wasn't taken over de facto either, but the military imposed its rule on politics. Parliament and the government no longer practised control over the country's weaponry.

With the coup, those liberal powers, socialist students, teachers, rural folk and labourers thought to have "become belligerent" were taken into custody and tortured. Even more significantly, the coup of 1971 went down in history due to three hangings. After their deaths, the people of Turkey came to know the three youths as *Denizler*, the plural form of one of their names. *Denizler* stood for a transformation of Turkey's collective imagination. The ghost of one of the youths, Deniz Gezmiş, will unexpectedly resurface in the later chapters of both this book and Turkey's history. First, let's take a look at the right-wing parliamentary members chanting "Three! Three! Three!" during the vote on the sentencing of the three youths in the General Assembly Hall on 24 April 1972. What are these men shouting about?

FASCISM OR DOWNRIGHT VENGEANCE?

We have already said that Turkey's adventure in the corruption of democracy and humanity goes way back in time. Since we have already begun travelling through time, let us go a little further back. What necessitates this is the right-wing parliamentary members' chanting of "Three! Three! Three!" on 24 April 1972, the day the vote on the death sentence of *Denizler* took place. Why three? Because there was yet another coup in 1960. Three hangings took three lives in the aftermath of this coup too, a coup that was perpetrated against the right-wing government by, it was said, "liberal military men". Incidentally, the coup of 1960 was referred to as a "revolution" rather than a coup for many years. In fact, the anniversary of the coup was celebrated as Liberty and Constitution Day. No amount of celebration and avoidance of the word "coup", however, could change the fact that 1960 took three lives as well. The right-leaning coup of 1971 therefore demanded three lives from the left to "get even", to wash away blood with blood. Just as the right-wing Prime Minister Adnan Menderes, Minister of Finance Hasan Polatkan and Minister of Foreign Affairs Fatih Rüştü Zorlu were executed in the coup of 1960, the play-off in 1971 also had to result in the taking of three lives. It did. Vengeance was had with the executions of Deniz Gezmiş, Yusuf Aslan and Hüseyin İnan, three youth leaders in their twenties. At the forefront of the right-wing parliamentary members who were out for blood to get even with the Left on 24 April 1972, chanting "Three! Three! Three!", was Süleyman Demirel, who would go on to say, "Yesterday is yesterday, today is today!" at

Cornell University years later. On that day, he was in Parliament, turning towards the seats of his party, shouting at them to approve the death sentence: "Raise your hands! Raise them!"

You decide if Turkey is a mouldering tree or one drying out after the constant pruning of bloody political retaliations. It's difficult to decide when the issue at hand is a chronicle of vendettas and the sides taking part have always judged one another according to enemy law. We can, however, still discuss the symbolic meanings of these milestones and the consequences they have had for Turkey.

* * *

But first, we need to go over the following dreary historical information.

After its founding in 1923, the Republic of Turkey was more or less ruled by Atatürk until his death in 1938. One can best get a sense of the era through a few of his adages:

"Turk: be proud, work, trust!"

"Blessed is he who calls himself a Turk!"

"We shall raise our national culture above the level of contemporary civilisation."

With the exception of the silenced dissidents, an entire nation worked and tamed its honour and pride through hunger, with the support of its founding father. This was a nation that was fresh out of a war in which it had lost everything, but Atatürk pointed to the light at the end of the tunnel with every goal he set, in every area of life. Among his maxims at the time, which covered just about every profession, is said to be, "Turkish drivers are people with the noblest of sensibilities."

You can picture the rest. Atatürk is a political figure who has permeated every aspect of Turkey, the entire consciousness of the nation, with not a single spot left untouched.

The years from 1938 to 1946, on the other hand, are known as the "National Chief" period. Atatürk's brother in arms and CHP (Republican People's Party) colleague İsmet İnönü was first Prime Minister and then President. Ever the "second man", İsmet İnönü's era coincides with World War II.

Forever associated with food stamps and political pressure, the "National Chief" period ended in 1946 when the first multi-party elections took place. The backlash against state-imposed modernism, one-party authority and heavy-handed statism was expressed through the right-leaning Democrat Party. Disregarding the first multi-party election in 1946, which wasn't very democratic, the first democratic election took place in 1950 and brought the Democrat Party to power. The Democrat Party's election slogan was the following sentence, underneath a hand raised as if to signal "stop":

"Enough! The people have their say!"

* * *

This meant that just twenty-seven years after the founding of the Republic, the "people" and the "state" diverged for the first time, Turkey claiming the high ground of democracy to prove its political maturity. The image of Turkey as a single entity walking the path set by Atatürk, collectively heading towards the goals set out in his declarations, was officially falling apart for the first time. The people were ahead of the state one–nil. The wind of liberty was blowing. Events, however, did not progress as expected, and far from keeping its promises of democracy, the party soon erected a right-wing centre of authority. In the end, Turkey's tradition of democracy would not allow for anything more than a hope for the best and a fear of the worst with each successive party. During its decade in power, the Democrat Party made Turkey a member of NATO (1952) and supported the incidents of 6–7 September 1955 when Istanbul minorities were lynched. With the administration's corruption and the rise of Islamic bigotry at their back, army officials staged the 1960 coup against the right-wing members of the administration: that is, against the Democrat Party. Atatürk's patriotic military men had "delivered the state and democracy from the people". The post-coup Constitution expanded the reach of constitutional rights and liberties. While the following decade saw the dissemination of left-wing movements, right-wing movements in turn grew more powerful thanks to the arms support of successive rightist administrations. Stuck between the USSR and the NATO member countries, Turkey became a stage on which the Cold War condensed and intensified. The coup of 1971 was justified by this chaos, but since no amount of effort could divert the masses from politics as effectively as intended, without an outlet the conflict spilled out onto the streets. The events of 1971–80 were an escalating civil war. And once religious denominations got involved, the bloodiest massacres of Turkey's history took place. Thirty-four people were killed on 1 May 1977. One hundred and fifty left-wing Alevis were killed in the Maraş Massacre of 1978 and another fifty-seven in the Çorum Massacre of 1980. Attacks against socialist students, teachers, workers and civil servants were so frequent that by the time the 1980s arrived, an average of twenty people were being killed every day. Between 1977 and 1980, 5,000 people lost their lives. Due to the intensity of events, both those who lived in Turkey during that era and those reading about this now might easily forget the fact that, in 1980, only fifty-seven years had passed since the founding of the nation. The consequences of the coup of 1980 – which, like its predecessors, was said to have been staged "to stop the war between brothers" – were as follows:

- The death penalty requested for 7,000 people
- 517 condemned to death
- Execution warrants for 259 sent to Parliament
- 49 executed
- 650,000 taken into custody
- 1,683,000 blacklisted
- 230,000 put on trial in 210,000 prosecutions
- 98,404 accused of the crime of "being an organisation member"
- 30,000 fired for being "objectionable"
- 388,000 denied passports
- The citizenship of 14,000 revoked
- 30,000 escaped abroad as political refugees
- 300,000 suspicious deaths
- 171 people's deaths from torture certified with documentation
- 14 deaths as a result of hunger strikes protesting against practices in prisons

- 937 films banned for being "objectionable"
- 23,667 associations banned from any activity
- The jobs of 3,854 teachers, 120 academics and 47 judges terminated
- 7,233 state functionaries exiled from their regions
- 9,400 either fired or exiled from public service
- Journalists sentenced to prison for a total of 3,315 years and 6 months
- Publishing of newspapers in Istanbul suspended for a total of 300 days
- 303 cases brought against 13 major newspapers
- Total prison sentences of 4,000 years sought against journalists
- 300 journalists assaulted and 3 killed
- 49 tons of newspapers, periodicals and books destroyed for being "objectionable".

So, this coup that took place just fifty-seven years after the founding of the Republic, what was its problem?

One way or another, and however much the rightist powers did their best to adapt to the fast-rising capitalism of the world, Turkey remained a mixed economy until the 1980s. There was nationalistic and left-wing resistance against the ruthlessness of capitalism. That was why, eight months before the coup of 12 September 1980, the notorious "24 January Economic Decisions" were made.

The national economy was to be subjected to an IMF-type programme. It would make possible the convertibility of the Turkish lira, the reduction of the public sector through privatisation, and the development of financial markets and establishment of capital markets. Import and export regulations were designed in order to liberalise foreign trade. Foreign capital was to be encouraged, interest rates liberalised, and flexible real exchange rate policies implemented. Capital levies and workers' fees would be reduced. Since none of this could happen with a strong and organised left-wing workers' movement in the country, the toll listed above had to take place. This was the reason why the 12 September 1980 coup was staged.

When CIA documents were made public decades later, it was established that right after the coup the CIA's Turkey station chief Paul Henze made a phone call to Jimmy Carter, the President of the USA at the time. Henze, his voice blaring from television screens in Turkey years later, had said that day: "Our boys did it!"

In the meantime, *our* educated, progressive, conscientious boys and girls perished in the torture chambers of Turkey. At the same time, all the coup generals who were responsible for this predicament, even the lowest-ranking ones, prepared to snag positions as board members or, at the very least, as consultants at multinational companies or in the national capital's largest conglomerates and go on with their lives.

Let us come finally to all that happened in Turkey's collective consciousness during this quite brief but excruciatingly long history, and what photographs and meanings were etched into that consciousness along with the twists and turns. Perhaps we may then be able to return to the original question that began this chapter and find an answer: is Turkey a tree that moulders due to bad planting or one drying up after the constant pruning of bloody political retaliations? Our reasons for attempting to recall and relate the past are so that we can try to unearth the past events that brought about today's mess, are they not? We are trying to understand where we stand in a history of vendettas. Aren't we?

TURKEY'S DISORGANISED PHOTO ALBUM

With his formidably muddled mind, home and story, Mr Turkey (I think we can all agree that he is a he) would like to show us his photo album. These are photographs of the memories and associations that have most deeply impressed and shaped him or have otherwise obsessed him, even though he cannot define them exactly. But the album is totally disorganised. Not only that, but a pile of photographs don't even fit inside it. Just as each attempt at organising a library is interrupted by a reverie as we come across a letter, a book, a journal or a note, Turkey too was interrupted each time he tried to organise his album and photographs of the past. The organised part of the album isn't even in chronological order. Why? Because "yesterday" doesn't stay put here. It oscillates between near and far in today's political, social and moral fights, conflicts and controversies. While a faraway memory appears fresh as a daisy, a very recent memory is treated as though *it happened a million years ago*. "But that's no way to perceive time," you say. "Doesn't that complicate things?" He replies, "It does complicate things. As it should!" You say,

"With yesterday at a constantly shifting distance, it must be easy to play games with people's memories." "Yes," he laughs. "Speaking of which, let me tell you a 'symbolic' and 'ironic' story about this whole mess." He tells the story of something that happened in April 2012 ...

* * *

"Ironic," read a tweet in April 2012. "In order to reach the courtroom to attend Kenan Evren's trial, you have to pass through Kenan Evren Boulevard, then Kenan Evren street." Still walking on the roads of a crippled democracy paved by the 1980 military coup, Turkey was about to witness the first symbolic trial of former generals Kenan Evren and Tahsin Şahinkaya. They were the members of the military responsible for the 1980 coup who were still alive. Both were absent due to poor health, and so was the public enthusiasm to question recent Turkish history. On 12 September 2010, the thirtieth anniversary of the 1980 coup, Turkey went to the polls to vote on a referendum for constitutional amendments. While some of the critical amendments involved changing the composition of high-level judicial entities in favour of the executive authority, the government touted the package of changes as a "great step forward in democracy". Their argument was that the perpetrators of the 1980 coup were to be tried and Turkey was to be reconciled with its recent bloody history. The 1980 coup was one of the cruellest in modern times, with 650,000 detentions, 230,000 prosecutions in military courts, and 300 deaths in prison, 171 of them the result of torture. There were forty-nine executions, including that of seventeen-year-old

Erdal Eren. Beyond the statistics of cruelty, the coup shaped the Turkish economy and established a minimum limit of 10 per cent of the total votes in a national election for any political party to be represented in Parliament.

During the public debate before the referendum, the opposition drew attention to the roots that the coup still has in the Turkish political and economic system. They argued that trying a few of the then military brass would not be enough to address the coup and its aftermath. As a response to that criticism, Prime Minister Erdoğan chose to give an emotional speech about young victims of the coup. His speech turned into a political game against the objectors, labelling them defenders of the coup. Finally, when the amendments were approved following the referendum, the impunity of the generals was abolished after forty years and Kenan Evren, the pasha, was called to stand trial. It was symbolically significant but equally inconsequential. Turkey waited for this magnificent trial for over a year.

4 April 2012 was the day when Kenan Evren, the pasha of blood and tears, was supposed to be in the courtroom. Due to a broken arm and health problems, he was not, but the co-plaintiffs in the case were there. One of them was 104-year-old Berfo, the mother of Cemil Kırbayır, who had disappeared during the coup. "I am here!" she said, from the ambulance in which she arrived, and she asked, "Where is Kenan Pasha?!"

The victims of the coup, once again carrying their pain in their hands, had been allowed to run after their oppressor only to see him slip away through their fingers again. The Progressive Lawyers' Association declared its recusal from the case.

They described it as a "show trial". So did many opponents on social media during the trial.

Almost everyone, including the harshest critics of the government, agreed that the trial was symbolically important but rejected the government's promotion of the case as the last frontier of democratisation. This is especially true when one considers that there have been thousands of political prisoners incarcerated under the Anti-terror Law, which is almost identical to the military laws of the 1980 coup. The critics of the government briefly argued that "back then, the label was the anarchist, now it is the terrorist".

* * *

During the trial, Twitter was awash with criticisms. One of them seemed to stand out, though. Özgür Mumcu, Associate Professor of Law, tweeted an article dating back to June 1981, almost one year after the 1980 coup. It was written by Matthew Rothschild in the *Multinational Monitor* and had the title "After the Tanks Come the Banks". The article was mainly about the miraculous economic success of Turkey after the coup:

> Turkey ranks as the third largest recipient of US military and economic aid behind Israel and Egypt. And US assistance is growing, with economic aid pledged to increase to US$350 million this fiscal year, compared to US$295 million last year. Military aid will show a 60 percent jump. For fiscal year 1981, the US gave US$250 million to Turkey in foreign military sales credits and

loan guarantees at about 4 percent below prime interest rate … Why the infusion of aid from the US? It "reflects our strong interest in a Turkey that's economically healthy and strong," says Larry Benedict, US State Department officer for Turkey. With the second largest NATO army (500,000 troops) and a foothold in the Middle East, Turkey counts as a crucial ally in the eyes of US policymakers. "Just look at its geographic position," says Benedict.

Reading the article, one cannot help but see the similarity to the international rhetoric on Turkey today. When you put together thousands of political prisoners with the "economic success of the Turkish model", it is not hard to understand why we are still passing along the Kenan Evren Boulevard. Just to see a symbolic trial for democratisation.

Most significant is the fact that Kenan Evren, the coup-monger with blood on his hands, never even passed Kenan Evren Boulevard to enter the courtroom. What's more, just before the case was brought against him, he had claimed, "I'll commit suicide if they prosecute me." Kenan Evren didn't commit suicide either.

Stunned, you stare at Mr Turkey and ask, "Is that really how it happened? Didn't the people rise up?" Once again he laughs. "If you wish, I can tell you how all crises in Turkey are seemingly solved through a small symbolic trick. But it might confuse you if I tell you now. It's best if we look through this photo album first. But when we're finished with the album, I'd love to introduce you to these mock conciliation tricks." All right, then. Let's take a look at the album. Let's pull out and examine at random Mr Turkey's pictures.

1. The Conquest of Istanbul: Fausto Zonaro's famous painting

Weren't we talking about the Republic of Turkey? So why are we going all the way back to the beginning of the Middle Ages, the Conquest of Istanbul? Because that date – and let me specify it to the day, 29 May 1453 – is one of the most vivid dates in Turkey's history. Because there is currently a populace in Turkey that feels itself to be increasingly Ottoman. For them, the nearest *yesterday*, the one they feel most attached to, is 29 May. They organise the biggest celebrations of the year on that date. The stadiums that were previously used for the 29 October celebrations, the anniversary of the founding of the Republic, now fill up on 29 May. In stadiums full to bursting, the Conquest of Istanbul is figuratively "re-enacted". On the green field, throngs of people in Ottoman attire and brandishing wooden swords attack men in Byzantine costumes. Although a few injuries occur every year due to bad acting or too much enthusiasm on part of the "symbolic" Ottoman soldiers, Istanbul is considered to have been conquered afresh when the Islamic or Ottoman flag is planted in the penalty box. Viewers chant in unison: "Allahu akbar! Allahu akbar!"

While the context is rather unclear, these conquest celebrations are often accompanied by collective judo and karate shows that are meant to be dazzling sports demonstrations. The appetite for conquest on the faces of the audience, on the other hand, is unbelievable. So much so that, even though they

conquer Istanbul anew every year, they soon become hungry again as if the city is never entirely theirs. Istanbul is a city that can never quite be conquered. For the same reason, enormous Turkish flags hang in various spots in Istanbul; in fact, you cannot take a single photograph of the Bosphorus without a Turkish flag in the frame. In spite of all the re-conquests, Istanbul is never Muslim enough, never Turkish enough, can never squeeze into its Sunni Turkish uniform as well as Anatolia does. But that undirected enthusiasm for the conquest! You would think that the masses crowded into the stadiums were heroic janissaries and not people with, say, fridge repayments at the centre of their small lives in their small neighbourhoods!

* * *

Yet in this picture from the album that we're looking at, Mehmet the Conqueror – that is, the actual person who conquered Istanbul with the Islamic flag – doesn't look at all excited, deranged, eager or passionate. He doesn't even yield a sword as he calmly rides a white horse through the city walls. You can see this painting in various coffee houses and offices in Turkey. There is another picture, one that lies in the pile outside the photo album. After the conquest, Mehmet the Conqueror is in calm conversation with the man who was the leader of Istanbul's Orthodox Patriarchate at the time. As told in the Ottoman history written by Alphonse de Lamartine, the Sultan himself sees the Patriarch to the door. If what they say is true, the Sultan in fact speaks in Romaic to the Patriarch. If you were to tell this to those in the stadiums who avidly consider themselves Ottoman, they wouldn't believe it, since it is not a stimulating enough tale to satisfy their zeal for the conquest. They prefer a yesterday that they themselves build with wooden swords and janissary marches to the actual pictures of history. That must be why the movie *Conquest 1453*, which came out in 2012, is the most watched film in Turkey's history. The strange thing is that when Devrim Evin, who played Mehmet the Conqueror, announced on Twitter that he could not make the Conquest celebrations of 2013 because he would be at the Gezi Park protests, he was found to be too real to play the Sultan and subsequently lynched on social media. But no one was angrier with the actor than the Istanbul Culture and Tourism Provincial Director, Professor Ahmet Emre Bilgili. Because he had brought together 500 students for the film screening whose names were Fatih – *conqueror* – Sultan and Mehmet! The meaning of Evin's first name, Devrim, however, was not conqueror but *revolution*.

Anyway, some in Turkey today feel that the Ottomans themselves weren't Ottoman enough. It's like when President Erdoğan claimed that the harem women in the TV series depicting Suleiman the Magnificent were too scantily clad and that sultans should be on expeditions rather than in their palaces. A joke photograph has been disseminated on social media for those who feel more Ottoman than the Ottomans. A photo showing the blond, European and extremely well-dressed members of the exiled Ottoman dynasty posing side by side is displayed alongside images of "Ottoman grandsons"

from Anatolia who are dark, Eastern and dressed in Islamic fashion. It has the title "Real Ottomans and Those Who Feel Ottoman", and it proves that rediscovered or revised history can never be the same as what happened in reality. A Mehmet the Conqueror who speaks Romaic and sees a priest to the door? Heaven forbid!

2. The map of Turkey: extremely sensitive borders

The poet Nazım Hikmet writes: "This land coming full gallop from the Far East, stretching into the Mediterranean like the head of a mare, is ours." He likens the shape of Anatolia to the head of a mare. It's easy to describe the contours of the country in verse, but when it comes to politics the quarrelling begins. I'm not sure if primary school students in other parts of the world are asked to draw their countries from memory, but my generation at the very least grew up copying the map of Turkey on the tissue paper dividing the pages of our drawing pads dozens of times in order to commit it to memory. Don't you leave out Hatay, close to the Syrian border! Don't skip over the little bumps and ridges in Thrace and let the Balkans snatch our land! Don't leave the Aegean islands to the Greeks! Be wary of Iran, Iraq and Armenia!

Throughout its history, Turkey's agenda was frequently gripped by anxiety about the contours of the map. The headlines of the papers covered frightening news with headlines such as: "Devious Map Uncovered!" In one example, Armenians were shown to have taken over part of the map for themselves; in another, the Kurds did the same. On a map leaked to the Turkish papers from a nationalistic meeting in

Greece, we had lost our islands; in a conspiracy theory implicating Syria, a piece of our land from *that* border disappeared.
The seeds of fear and anxiety had been planted when Turkey's
borders were first drawn. As the director Nuri Bilge Ceylan
said in his acceptance speech at Cannes, the children of this
"lonely and beautiful country" were raised on the cliché that
was used to describe the map:

"Surrounded by enemies …"

Another cliché used for years was "Turkey's strategic
position", which implied both a source of anxiety and political
opportunity. In terms of the people living on the borders, the
map was pregnant with all sorts of tragic, bizarre or colourful
stories. Every year, without fail, a variation on the same picture
graces the papers during religious holidays. The headline is
always the same: "Merry holidays on the border!"

In the eastern and south-eastern regions, people on either
side of the wire fence throw gifts and extend hands to one
another. People lined up on either side of the fence lay out

tables and raucously exchange holiday pleasantries. In the west
– that is to say the islands – Turkish-speaking friends and relatives arrive from Greece to converse in coffee houses. Markets
are set up.

"Strategic importance" carries no weight at these meetings.
There are only families and friendships divided by the drawing
of the borders. In Izmir in the west, when people drink rakı,
after their second glass they start raising them towards the
lights in Greece; they keep marvelling, "It's so near." These
unofficial photos aren't in the album, naturally. In particular,
the hundreds of overturned trucks on the hard shoulder of
the road running from the Iranian border towards Turkey are
never seen in the official album. Why do these trucks lie there
like that? So that contraband diesel from Iran can be siphoned
out of their tanks before they arrive in the city. These trucks
that look like they have laid their heads down on the rocks in
their misery speak volumes about how defined and yet how
tenuous are Turkey's borders.

Yet sometimes our closest neighbours are the most distant
from us. On either side of the Armenian border are cannons
symbolically pointing towards each other. Even though
Armenia is full of cheap goods from Turkey and women from
Armenia are often hired as nannies in Turkey, the borders are
still thick and decisive. Turkey's map, its passport photo, is as
deficient and lacklustre as any one of our own photographs.

3. Letters, hats, attire …: the models of the Republic

After reading an article as a teenager on the attractiveness of
Atatürk as a man, I wondered: "Is Atatürk handsome?"

I realised I couldn't say. No matter how hard I try, I cannot see Atatürk as a person, as a man. There's an enormous obstacle in the way of my perception. When you see pictures of a figure that often, from morning till night, starting at primary school and going right up until the end of university, it becomes almost completely impossible to think of him as a man, as a person. My generation and the ones that came after, at least, have seen Atatürk so often that we have forgotten he was a person. Photos notwithstanding, and especially after the coup of 1980, we have seen so many statues of him on high pedestals that it's impossible to even imagine him being the size of a normal person. Let's pick three out of the hundreds of photographs we have memorised.

The first is Atatürk at a blackboard, presenting the new alphabet. With a piece of chalk he introduces the letters of the Latin alphabet to the nation. Those who, like me, had to learn the Arabic alphabet prior to the alphabet reform doubtless are the most thankful to Atatürk for this. It's right to remember the alphabet reform with cheers and appreciation as it is perhaps the most important part of the cultural revolution that commenced with the founding of the Republic, yet the fact remains that a people's bond to its past was severed in a single night. I'm talking about grandchildren who couldn't read letters from their grandfathers, people who couldn't understand wills and land titles dating back to the Ottoman era, people who were unable to read old poetry or even love letters found in the attic. I can go on for pages about the void this created in the collective consciousness, but this one example should suffice.

To make money, children in Tehran sell old poems on pink tissue paper the size of bus tickets. The love poems of Fuzuli, one of my favourite poets of the Ottoman era, are among the most popular of these. I remember buying from a child in Tehran the following poem written in Persian, only to stare blankly at it:

Enhance my lover's beauty all the more
As for me, make me even more lovesick for her.

Feeling sorry for me, the eight-year-old read me the poem. Is it possible for a people who cannot read its own love poems to have a history of love? I wonder what it would be like if a German couldn't read Goethe or an Englishman stared blankly at the sonnets of Shakespeare. A Turk who cannot read Fuzuli is more or less the same thing.

Another photo in the album that engenders the same zeal is from the time of the hat reform.

The most popular Grand Bazaar purchase of tourists visiting Istanbul today is the fez, but the fez hasn't been worn in Turkey since 1925. Speaking of which: apple tea is just as un-drunk in Turkey as the fez is unworn. I have no idea what marketing genius planted it in the minds of visitors to Istanbul, but every tourist coming into the country instantly becomes an apple tea addict. However, apple tea is only ever sold in souvenir shops and duty free stores at the airport. I think someone has to speak out!

Introduced by Atatürk on 27 August 1925 with the words, "This headgear is known as the hat," the hat entered Turkey's

life in a single day while the remaining Eastern styles of head and general attire were banned. Europeans might remember it from Saint-Exupéry's *The Little Prince*. It is a Turkish astronomer who discovers the asteroid where the Little Prince lives (B612). The astronomer presents his findings at an international conference, but no one listens to him due to his fez and Eastern clothes. Following a Turkish dictator's clothing reform, which forces everyone to dress like Europeans, the same astronomer participates in the conference, this time in modern clothes, and the audience is convinced. This section of *The Little Prince*, which is well known by European readers, is rather unfamiliar in Turkey. For, due to this excerpt that mocks Atatürk and his clothing reform, until recently Turkish readers have had to read a censored version of the book.

Why, then, is this photograph from the album – a photo that has affected even *The Little Prince* – so significant for Turkey? Why do we pick out this photograph of Atatürk pointing at a hat rather than a photograph of the War of Independence that was the nation's salvation?

This is a hat that is more significant than it appears, that's why. Like Rene Magritte's pipe, the hat Atatürk holds in his hand in the photos "n'est pas une chapeau"! It's like a tiny picture of a shard of this country's spirit. Just as the Alphabet Reform illustrates an extensive past being abandoned in favour of a bright future, so the Hat Reform is the image of the separation of religion and state.

Eighteen people were executed in various parts of Turkey for opposing the Hat Law that became effective in 1925, while many were imprisoned or exiled. Public servants, for whom it was mandatory to wear hats, were given "hat advances" so they could buy them. During the days when a hat advance was 80 liras, a loaf of bread cost 5 *kuruş*. That meant 1,600 loaves of bread bought one hat. You can hear thousands of tragic stories about cultural revolutions from countries that were modernised forcibly by their governments. But the interesting thing here was the effort to package the people who had joined in defending their country in head coverings, fezzes, turbans and kerchiefs and had sacrificed their sons and daughters to the war. Imagine yourself as a half-starved Republic-defending public servant who had returned from the war three years earlier. I would expect your story with the hat to be no less dark and tragic than the one about Gogol and the coat. In the same way that Russian literature is purported to have sprung from Gogol's coat, the myriad absurd tragedies experienced in Turkey today sprang from this hat. A tradition that is "rediscovered" or "resurgent" cannot be said to be the same as the one that existed before. It comes laden with a gradually increasing feeling of resentment. That was why the hat returned to Turkey's agenda in the 1990s and early 2000s. This time around, the hat was a symbol of pro-Atatürk women who defended Western values against Islamic conservatism. One could identify "secular aunties", whose presence continues today, by their hats. In today's Turkey, these aunties are akin to retired clerks still celebrating 1 May in post-USSR Russia. They are the heroes of an obsolete social project trying to prove that it still exists.

The banned turban, Islamic attire and – last but definitely not least – the headscarf struck back hard from the 1980s onwards. And they struck back as the most potent symbols of Turkey's cultural crisis. The fedora in Atatürk's hand, as you know, is no longer carried by anyone except for old grandfathers on their holidays. At homes in Turkey where a wake is being held, a pair of the deceased's shoes is left outside the front door. It's a mournful sight. Left outside the door of Turkey's cultural and social chaos today, if you ask me, is a fedora.

Here is a photograph of the first woman in Turkey to obtain a driver's licence, Mevhibe İnönü, better known as the wife of the second man of the Republic, "National Chief" İsmet İnönü. Mevhibe *Hanım* was such a diminutive woman that people are surprised when they see her clothes exhibited at her villa. Now and then, at the Pink Villa in Ankara where İsmet and Mevhibe İnönü lived, an exhibition is held on the details of their life there. Should you visit, you can see Mevhibe *Hanım*'s Alice in Wonderland-sized shoes and dresses. They are all of the Western fashion of the time. According to the interview I did with her daughter, however, Mevhibe *Hanım* was tremendously uncomfortable when she first wore these Western clothes and didn't want to uncover her head; she only reluctantly acquiesced later in order to fulfil her duty to set an example for Turkey. Mevhibe *Hanım* is neither the first woman to be used as a display window mannequin for social projects nor the last. As a matter of fact, the substitution of women as the modelling clay of social and political projects has been widespread throughout the world and continues to be so. For a contrary instance, Turkey's current first lady, Emine Erdoğan, has said in an interview (later disclaimed) that she was beaten by her brother the first time her family forced her to wear a headscarf.

Our reason for looking at Mevhibe *Hanım*'s photographs in the album is not to bring up the artificiality of state-imposed modernisation or to criticise the Republic over it, which is virtually a cliché by now. Nor is the issue here to expose the harsh nature of the oppression that countered the social reaction to these regulations. The point is that issues of Westernisation and modernity, since the very beginning, have been made synonymous with putting women on display and dressing and undressing them. These old photographs are at the root of discussions about an entire identity crisis and the duality of miniskirts versus headscarves even today. Even worse than this is the folly of pretending or presuming that the "tension over miniskirts versus headscarves" has been solved. In fact, the Republic is represented neither by the hat-wearing secular "women" nor the Islamic nouveau riche "ladies" in Versace and Gucci, as we shall see in the "Today" section of this book. Let me also mention in passing that the words "woman" and "lady" also indicate a political divergence in present-day Turkey. While use of the word *woman* has been jettisoned to the seculars as a near-eroticisation, the status of *ladyhood* is a privilege reserved exclusively for headscarf-wearing women. Naturally, there are endless tricks up the sleeve of a country that uses women as jokers in the pack of cards of its social projects. We'll come to that later.

4. Boy towers and girl marching bands

These are the first photographs of the newly founded Republic that will be repeated in various ways throughout the following decades. One shows a human tower formed in a stadium on 19 May by young men climbing onto one another's shoulders. Let's leave aside the fact that 19 May, the day the War of Independence began, which is celebrated annually as the Youth and Sports Day, is symbolised by such a phallic image. Instead, let's examine the girls. Just like the boys, they are dressed all in white and brandish trumpets as they march back and forth

in military step through the same streets in every city every year. As one of the finest writers in the Turkish language, Sevgi Soysal, pointed out in a flawless newspaper article in the late 1960s, they also wear spotless white gloves. These young women and men march decisively in their immaculate white clothes into a bright future and erect their towers in defiance of gravity. When the stadiums fill to bursting with students from every school, everyone puts on their own show. Girls dance in shorts. They form a large picture with their bodies on the green field, often either the Turkish flag or the map – and if not that, then the signature of Atatürk.

Afghanistan today tends to be depicted through photographs of women when making comparisons between the past and the present. Pictures of women in burkas are presented next to those of Afghani women in miniskirts in the 1960s. Similar comparisons were made for Iran in the 1990s. We have no way of knowing how representative such old photographs were of ordinary people of the time, whether wearing miniskirts was a privilege accessible only to the upper classes, as it is now, but a similar faulty comparison can be made with these 19 May photographs from the 1940s. For as Turkey gradually grew more conservative, the shorts worn by the girls in these celebration day images soon became below-the-knee skirts, and then modern-looking harem pants. From an outside perspective, the coup of 1980 was equated with secularism, but it was the first step in this retrogression, decreeing that girls wear longer skirts to school. At the same time as it was killing university students in torture chambers, it filled stadiums with these youths in snow white to demonstrate "the eternal sunshine of the spotless mind". Once a display performed for the noblest of sentiments – the whitest/purest/most spotless youth and the powers of the Republic at their fittest – the 19 May celebrations were soon considered obsolete. In order to make them valid, they even devolved into activities where pop music was played and the girls performed gyrations akin to belly dancing. The most significant moment of this transformation or regression came when, in the early years of the escalating tension between secularism and conservatism, girls danced to a remix of the Tenth Anniversary March by a pop performer. The track was played in clubs for years afterwards, with apolitical white Turk youths throwing their hands in the air and howling along in an outpouring of secularist sentiment.

The saddest part is that a youth "stripped of ideology" was left no choice but to cling to and defend this kind of obsolete ritual when faced with Islamic conservatism. Likewise, in the 2000s, the secular faction of society could no longer find any symbol with which to defend their lifestyles other than the Turkish flag and the portrait of Atatürk. For this neutered secular rhetoric, we owe much to the coup and Constitution of 1980, which prohibited all political symbols and words!

5. The photograph of a bearded man who said, "This is a shame, it is a sin, it is cruelty"

We have two images here. One is the plaintive face of a man with a long, dark beard. The other shows a triumphant young female pilot. Before I explain what these two photographs from 1937 are doing side by side in the album, let me tell you about a poem.

In Turkey, every teenager, and to some extent everyone else – even if they have no interest in poetry – knows this poem:

"Now you are leaving / go / and what then of your eyes! / They leave too, of course ..."

This is a poem by famed "love poet" Cemal Süreya. His name is misspelled in Turkish, for he lost one of the two ys of Süreyya in a bet with a poet friend! He's a facetious man, famous for the humour in his poetry. Of this, he has said, "perhaps humour is something created in me by the attempt to avoid profanity. That certainly seems to be the case when I think back to my childhood days. The wish to save things from humiliation. To make light of things."

Neither that humiliation nor this poem of his is as well known:

I opened my eyes on a freight wagon / Onto a truck they loaded us / In the sentry of two privates with rifles / Along with those two privates they loaded us onto the freight wagon / In a village they dumped us after days of voyage / As prehistoric dogs barked / Never have I forgotten that voyage, the barking, policemen / My sensibility, perhaps,

thrives on those childhood impressions too / My mother died in exile, my father died in exile.

The poet Cemal Süreya is in fact one of the victims of the Dersim Massacre and exile that took place in 1937–38. The photographs of the bearded man and young female pilot I mentioned above belong to these years, this massacre. The bearded man is the Alevi Kurdish leader Seyit Riza, leader of the revolt. The Republic chose Atatürk's adopted daughter Sabiha Gökçen, the young pilot in the photo, to lead the bombing of the "mutinous" people of Dersim. What remains of the massacre that left an estimated 90,000 people dead are the Sabiha Gökçen airport on the Anatolian side of Istanbul and the words of Seyit Rıza, "This is a shame, it is a sin, it is cruelty," uttered just before he was hanged and buried in a location still unknown. Following the exile from Dersim, various Alevi Kurdish villages were established west of Turkey "for unknown reasons".

* * *

Seyit Rıza, the most prominent figure among those who refused to wear the Sunni Turk uniform designed for them by the Republic, also said, in relation to the administration of the time: "I could not put up with your lies, which have been the source of my troubles. I did not kneel down before you, and may that be the source of your troubles." Sabiha Gökçen, who dropped the first bomb on Dersim from her plane, said in an interview years later: "One feels absolutely no pity dropping bombs on a live target. One only thinks of one's duty, of tracking and striking it." Seyit Rıza's final words are still repeated today as a conscientious slogan in opposition to state violence. This was quite possibly the sentence that was shared most often in the wake of the killing of the boys in the Gezi uprising:

"This is a shame, it is a sin, it is cruelty!"

After Seyit Rıza's death and the suppression of the revolt, Dersim's name was changed to Tunceli; however, this did not prevent people from being detained and tortured if their birthplace was listed as Tunceli on their identification cards. In Turkey today, if you speak to someone who refers to her city as Dersim rather than Tunceli, know that it is Seyit Rıza she reveres, not Sabiha Gökçen. And although the subject is spoken of in hushed voices in Turkey, it is still extremely vivid. In the highly controversial news article published by Armenian journalist Hrant Dink in his newspaper *Agos* before he was killed on 19 January 2007, it was alleged that Sabiha Gökçen had been one of the children spared in the Armenian deportation. There are those who claim that this news article is among the reasons why Hrant was killed. That a child who was the victim of one massacre has grown up to be a bomber in another ... yes, the pure historical tragedy of the situation stretches the limits of credulity.

6. A village boy playing the mandolin

In Turkey, no one cries easily anymore over unfortunate, distressing or horrible things. Perhaps it's because we're so used to such things that we all find it easy to fix our face and our spirits; we're not so easily caught off guard. Instances of beauty tend to be more able to elicit tears. This 1940 photograph of a skinny, split-shoed yet cheerful village boy playing the mandolin, for example.

How avid his attention to his mandolin, how hopeful and how sincere his belief in life. Is it the fact that his hope will soon disappear and that such children have always been let down that makes our eyes fill

with tears? The year is 1940 ... skinny, bald-headed and huge-eyed village children with tiny bodies build their own schools, plant their own trees and bestow upon Turkey's history a miracle that will be only too brief. At their head, the man who familiarised Turkey with world classics, Minister of Education Hasan Ali Yücel. Who is this man who scurries about with such urgency?

"As soon as he comes he is leaving / Always, always in a hurry."

This is how Can Yücel, arguably the most foul-mouthed yet brilliant poet in the Turkish language, described his father Hasan Ali Yücel in a poem about him. He was the founder of the "village institutes", the loss of which will always be remembered with sorrow in Turkey's history. The village institutes, which performed miracles in the country's history and aimed to give the finest education to poor, promising rural children in order for them to become village teachers, lasted only six years. The problem was political. According to some historians, the changing balance en route to the Cold War made the survival of such schools impossible, since they cultivated "people with a communist spirit". In 1947, girls and boys in the village institutes were separated. The same year, a public mandate decreed that translations of world classics be collected and burned. In 1948, the institutes were converted into regular schools, effectively losing their function. In 1954, under the administration of the right-wing Democrat Party, they were shut down altogether. However, even in the six short years of their existence, they performed their ordained function and bequeathed Turkey a singular generation. The village institutes continue to be remembered with sadness today.

Now let's move on to why, out of all the village institute students who played the violin, piano, trumpet or harmonica, I've picked the one with the mandolin. It's ironic. Although the institutes were shut down, the mandolin maintained its place in Turkey's primary education. Children playing the mandolin and singing were an unchanging part of the 23 April National Independence and Children's Day. That is, until the coup of 1980. The coup stuffed recorders into the mouths of the singing children, subjecting all primary school children

in Turkey ever since to those plastic flutes. Starting with my generation, this transformation eventually eradicated the children who had once paraded through the streets playing the mandolin and singing. The coup popped a whistle into our mouths that we would play for years to come. The mandolins were removed, never to be seen again.

7. The metal cauldron with the USA flag, Hollywood-esque wedding photographs and "Japanese–Chinese thingamajig"

The following, apparently unrelated, photographs depict the transformation of Turkey between the years 1950 and 1960 and actually have a lot to do with one another. But let's just say first that the whole story came out of a metal cauldron. The inscription on it reads, in broken Turkish:

"To Turk people from people of United States of America"

Underneath the inscription are two hands in a handshake. Yet one of the hands seems to be gripping the other more tightly, as though it won't let it go.

The container, according to what's written on it, is filled with "plain powdered milk". Another photograph shows children, the second generation of the Republic, laughing as they sit at their school desks and drink a mixture of water and powdered milk from copper cups. Their joy is due to being children of a nation that is receiving the American Marshall Plan aid given to countries whose economies have been ravaged by World War II thanks to the political acrobatics of Prime Minister Adnan Menderes, despite not having participated in the war.

They are unaware of what it will cost them, and that in twenty-five years' time, as retribution for the cost, they will

receive the "Japanese–Chinese thingamajig" planted in a now forgotten part of the capital: the Korean Veterans Memorial. A gift from South Korea for the men Turkey lost in the Korean War.

The Korean War – which Turkey almost never mentions, despite the pride it takes in its militarism and heroism – was the cost of the famous Marshall Plan aid that is remembered by the generation who had to pinch their noses shut to drink the powdered milk. The soldiers in this three-year war – a war Turkey had to participate in due to being part of NATO forces – returned with Vietnam syndrome, becoming alcoholic or depressed, and were almost never spoken of. No one would listen to the heroism of soldiers injured while fighting someone else's war.

In those days, a consequence of the Marshall Plan was that railway construction was stopped and replaced by highway construction. As all four corners of Turkey were rapidly connected, the roads were most frequently used to bring

Hollywood films to Anatolian towns, the first generation of the Republic filling the newly constructed movie theatres. No one had time to listen to the Korea veterans, because the movie was about to begin! It was in those days that it became fashionable for newlyweds to go to photographers' studios to dress up like Greta Garbo and Humphrey Bogart and have their picture taken. Everyone started to resemble the guys and dames in the movies a little. The roads taking Hollywood movies to Anatolian towns simultaneously enabled the first migration of the Republic from those towns to the cities of Istanbul and Ankara. Having resolutely sided with the USA in the Cold War, Turkey was speeding away from its goal of a "fully independent Turkey" in terms of both its economy and its social life. As an example, the aeroplane factory in Eskişehir that was ready to start production was abandoned in favour of imports from the USA. Despite consolidating the "demand for liberty" against the oppressive policies of the one-party era, the Democrat Party soon built its own autocracy through political and press bans. The "crowds" were in power now. The Islamic religion and call to prayer, which had been made Turkish with the founding of the Republic, were now converted back to Arabic, the "crowds" gratefully reuniting with their religion – just the way they liked it. Those same crowds, however, wouldn't accept the fact that the populist Prime Minister Adnan Menderes, himself a land baron, had rescinded the law that would allow village folk to own land and stopped railway construction at the request of the USA. The novelist Kemal Tahir succinctly described the massive transformation of Turkey in the 1950s as follows:

"The scholarly and educated folk had always reigned over the people, until the 1950s that is."

Meanwhile, the photographs of one night in 1955 are among the best hidden in the album. With the provocation of the right-wing pro-administration press, the homes and offices of non-Muslims were looted during the night of 6–7 September. The tragicomic part of it was that "communists" were blamed for the racist nocturnal pillaging set in motion by the right-wing administration, leading to the arrests of hundreds of socialists starting the next day.

"The scholarly and educated folk" would wait for around ten years to retaliate …

8. 555K and the left fist

A cryptic inscription on the walls of Ankara, the capital, in May 1950:

555K

What does it mean? Only the young people who have quietly systematised their fury know the answer. The "scholarly and educated" youths meet up on the 5th day of the 5th month at 5 pm in Kızılay to oppose Prime Minister Adnan

Menderes, who came to power with promises of liberty. They chant, "We want liberty!"

On that day, Menderes in turn drives his own young supporters to the square. The lyrics to a march from the Ottoman era are changed and sung by the protesters:

"How can this be? / How can brothers shoot one another? / Blasted dictators / Do you really think you can inherit this world?"

* * *

On 27 May 1960, just twenty-two days after the movement is started by the youth and scholars, young officers seize control of the government.

There is a photograph taken in 1960 on the 5th day of the 5th month at 5 pm in Ankara. What are most apparent are two left fists raised in the air. It looks like a new thing, but this protest is in fact utilising references to the War of Independence. Just like then, the *Kuvayi Milliye* (National Forces) once again rise to defend the nation against imperialist powers in the leadership of the "people's educated scholars". At least, that's

how it is in the imaginations of the people gathered there. But then these two left fists … In droves, the Turkish people begin to acquaint themselves with left-wing ideology and Marxism. Although among the youth Atatürk and the War of Independence are still a fresh reference for an anti-imperialist attitude, the masses are finally becoming aware of socialist ideology. On the other hand, it is also in these times that Turkey begins to lose its reverence for "scholarly and educated folk". Times when people start saying, "Overactive minds are soon filled with terrible ideas …"

9. Hands, fists and the unending handshake

On 3 June 1963 in Moscow, a man left his second-floor apartment, went to the newsstand and reached for his daily newspaper. No sooner had he picked up the paper than his hand went slack and he collapsed. Nazım Hikmet, that colossal poet of the Turkish language, who was imprisoned for twelve years because of his poems, forced to flee his country in the final years of his life and ultimately punished by denaturalisation, died a quick and graceful death to match the magnificence of his life.

Surely during those same days a young teacher in a village in Anatolia, who had learned the power of literature by reading the world classics that Hasan Ali Yücel had translated in training school, reproduced by hand and in candlelight the banned poems of Nazım Hikmet. There were other hands, too. Young men who attended university in suits and ties, young women in skirt suits, research assistants who went hungry half the time, young lawyers, young farmers … the first patriotic, intellectual youth fostered by the Republic banded together

under the freedom of speech and organisation granted by the 1961 Constitution. Fists were raised over tables in genuine and sincere belief in the first article of the 1961 Constitution, which had come with the promise of freedom:

"The Turkish Nation hereby enacts and proclaims this Constitution drafted by the Constituent Assembly of the Turkish Republic, and entrusts it to the vigilance of her sons and daughters who are devoted to the concepts of freedom, justice and integrity, with the conviction that its basic guarantee lies in the hearts and minds of her citizens."

The devoted and vigilant sons and daughters ask: how can a fully independent nation be formed with a foreign-dependent economy, village folk without their own land and workers without humane living conditions?

The left fists that steadily grew in number as the talking hands were raised wanted to shake free from the too-tight grip of the USA as shown on the powdered milk containers. The village folk without land wanted land, mine workers wanted their rights, and students wanted the American soldiers who had docked in Izmir port in 1968 with Vietnam's blood on their hands to leave our territory immediately.

By the end of the 1960s, Nazım Hikmet's poems were being published and read, and in 1965 Haldun Taner's play "I Shut My Eyes and Do My Duty" was performed on stage for the first time. That play has the choir shouting: "Overactive minds soon fill with terrible ideas!"

"Overactive minds", in the form of village folk being led by students, seized land from land barons and student associations turned into operational political establishments, thus raising the poet's hand that had fallen in Moscow one morning. The 1960s in Turkey were as poetic and deserving of a mythology as they were in Europe. There was a tomorrow and it was bright ... until the picture appeared of a tall, handsome young man between two policemen.

10. Tarzan, philosophy and the book with the holes

Years before Johnny Weissmuller yodelled and swung from branches in the movie *Tarzan*, a man in the city of Manisa in the west of Turkey lived in the forest in only a pair of shorts and talked to no one but joined in every official parade in the city wearing a War of Independence medallion over a palm leaf on his chest. Do films imitate life or is it the other way around?

The people of Manisa only thought to call him the Tarzan of Manisa after first viewing the movie *Tarzan* in the 1950s. Ahmet Bedevi – which was his given name – almost single-handedly breathed life into the forests of Manisa after they were ravaged by fire during the war. It is still a point of intrigue that he was able to clamber up the mountains of Manisa in bare feet in a just few minutes, and ceremonies are held each year on the anniversary of his death at his statue in the city. No one really asks this one question, however. What did the man see in the war that caused him to become completely mute? Why was he left to grow an entire forest on

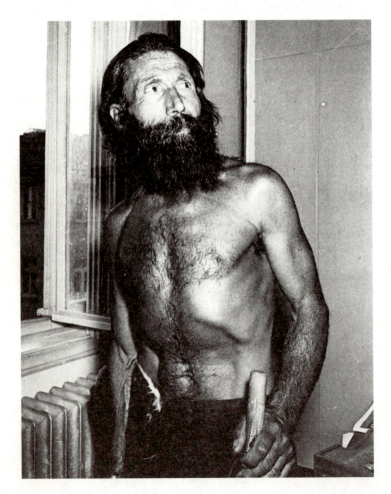

his own without a single helping hand? Would a statue have been erected in this very dark-skinned man's honour if not for the movie *Tarzan*? Still, after the poem written by the realist and obstinate daydreamers of 1960s' Turkey, and perhaps after the movies are over, Tarzan passes away in 1963 and real life begins. A life summed up by this sentence:

"The ubiquitous triumph of the proletariat is not a utopia but a belief founded in objectivity."

An orange book percolates among the youth of the nation: *Elementary Principles of Philosophy* by Georges Politzer. This is the holy book for all literate young people since 1966. The sweet ascension of the left throughout the 1960s, however, is oppressed with each new obstacle erected by the state and grows exponentially more stubborn. By the time the 1970s come around, a new book can be seen in the hands of the young: the Book with Three Holes! Known by this name in Turkey, the cover shows the slogan "Viva la *Revolución!*" Half-concealed by three bullet holes. So people ask for it in bookstores as:

"The Book with Three Holes!"

The main subject of discussion among the youth is no longer the particulars of dialectic materialism but whether revolutionary armed struggle will move from the cities to the villages or from the villages to the cities.

Roughly fifty years after the founding of the Republic, the "scholarly, educated folk" will attempt armed revolt. With the 1971 memorandum, Deniz Gezmiş and his two friends, Hüseyin İnan and Yusuf Aslan, whose faces I would like you to remember, are hanged to be made an example of. That's who it is in the photograph of the tall, handsome young man between

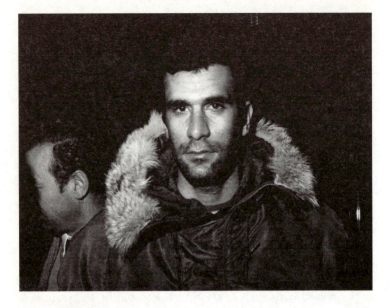

the two policemen: Deniz Gezmiş. Years later, too, we shall encounter it again.

These young hangings are a milestone for Turkey. Known to imprison and constantly harass its scholars, for the first time the Republic has hung three youths through its representatives in Parliament. It has done this for all to see and has opened the gates of Hell. The hanging of three youths who walked the path paved by the National Forces changed the face of the state in the minds of the masses. From that day on, being young in Turkey became synonymous with being "possible suspects". Also from that day on, the associations with Atatürk divided into two: an "anti-left", uniformed, calcified totality of ideologies defended by the army on the one hand; and a left-leaning patriotism with the ideology of "total independence" at its centre on the other. The latter is apparent in Deniz Gezmiş's final defence prior to his hanging.

The prosecutor says: "These men don't speak of Atatürk, all they do is imitate Mustafa Kemal's fur-collared picture." The mention of the fur collar and his first name suggests Atatürk's incarnation as a revolutionary before the founding of the state. The prosecutor is right: the hanged youths refrain from using the name Atatürk, which, after the state's founding, became symbolic of the oppressive regime and was appropriated by the army. These youths, whose activism had started against the Sixth Fleet of the US Navy at the same port where the first shot was fired against the Greek forces besieging Izmir during the War of Independence, have taken it upon themselves to wage war just like "Mustafa Kemal" had done. For them, there is little distance between Che Guevara and Mustafa Kemal. This fissure and divergence is one that is still valid in Turkey. The great fracture in Turkey's collective consciousness developed on 6 May 1972 at Ulucanlar Prison in the small hours of the morning. A dove was said to have taken flight – according to their lawyers – from the prison courtyard the day the three youths were hanged.

11. Fatsa Children's Choir, the logo of the Meat and Fish Institution, the bone age document

Children sing in a tiny town in the Black Sea region, chins raised to make themselves heard. Fatsa, May 1980. Intellectuals invited from Istanbul are about to start writing accolades about the fully democratic, fair and just life built in this near-communal little town that is being scapegoated by the government. Right now, they listen to the children laugh and gesticulate entertainingly as they sing this song:

I went to the market looking for bread / They said it cost more, I was dismayed / They had fat bellies, I was left squat / What should I do, where should I go? / It was the cheapest, how can I make do?

I went to the market looking for the people / At the resistance, they said, I was delighted / Workers and village folk alike march as I gape / What should I do, where should I go? / My people are at the resistance, with them I must go.

I went to the market with my rifle / With my workers and village folk I look for the fat bellies / The robbers run as I chase them down / What should we do, where should we go? /On the path to power we must walk together.

* * *

Revolutionary Way, the most active leftist organisation in the country, presents the nation with an exemplary left-wing administration with its first term in mayorship. Meanwhile, left-leaning Alevi citizens in various cities of Anatolia are being massacred, but the most worrisome news in the papers is about Fatsa. For the footsteps of the left, steadily growing stronger throughout the 1970s, ring loudest from this little town. The progressive intellectuals write about Fatsa with enthusiasm. One especially situates the town in terms of humanity's history:

"What I saw in Fatsa was a different social life. It is observed that the people of Fatsa possess characteristics and values that have been lost or are being lost in the current process of modernisation, not to be replaced. Fatsa manifests the hope that seemingly irresolvable social dilemmas can indeed be solved when people are given the right to exercise free will over decisions pertaining to their own lives. On behalf of the age we are in, I would like to thank the people of Fatsa."

So sociologist Ünsal Oskay ends his article, and just a month later the local government of Fatsa, the first concrete achievement of the rising left in the country, is raided by government forces on the grounds that "they are building a government against the government". Men in ski masks hustle an entire town into building the Meat and Fish Institution and then torture them. Not even the members of the Fatsa Children's Choir are spared. All this adequately horrifies no one, however. The course of events set in motion by the three executions in 1972 has already seen thousands of people imprisoned and tortured. Everyone – including children – is a political subject. Every one of the largest cities is a Beirut. The cities are divided district by district, street by street. The "fascist commandos", armed and blatantly

supported by the rightist authorities, patrol the streets while leftist militants guard themselves and their neighbourhoods with whatever weapons they can get their hands on. Martial law has been in effect in several provinces for the past few years. Political assassinations operate in an arithmetic of "one from the right, then one from the left". In the final two years of the 1970s, Alevi citizens start being massacred; in the cities where this takes place, a few days preceding each incident there are inexplicable sightings of American lottery ticket vendors! Finally, military boots march into this little town on the Black Sea coast.

A few months after the "Point Operation" of July 1980, the first sign appears of the coup that will come in September and will leave the subsequent period of Turkey's history in twilight. It punctuates the sentence of the Fatsa Children's Choir and begins another, never-ending:

"The Republic of Turkey is an indivisible whole in and of its country and people … blah blah blah blah … in these days when we need national unity and integrity … blah blah …"

A general, whose face we will be seeing constantly throughout the following years, speaks these words on state TV on the morning of 12 September. For days, whenever the general vanishes from the screen, the same folk song starts playing:

"Once more it rears up, the foreman's white horse | It seems time for us to set out to the borders | Beat on the drums *aman aman* | It seems time for us to set out to battle *aman* | We set out to the borders | Now and then we must set out, set out on a crusade | When fall comes by, oh fond we are of spring |

Our rose-cheeked maidens, oh we love by guile / Military men, oh, cannot but set out."

* * *

I suppose my mention of the prevailing vividness of Mehmet the Conqueror's picture in the first pages of the photo album makes more sense when you know that this janissary march from the Ottoman era provides the representative sound for the coup of 12 September. The lesson to be learned from the folk song that replaced the Fatsa Children's Choir for good is this:

"The Turkish army has started crusading, cannot do without crusading. And it knows to love its maiden / that is, the nation / even if by guile!"

A tragicomic detail is that the artist who performed this song, Hasan Mutlucan, is said to have died of chagrin because, although he was a socialist, his voice came to be associated with the coup. Despite the fact that for years the artist had declared his opposition to the coup, this folk song – along with his voice – was the soundtrack to documentaries about the coup for generations. He is among the unfortunate millions whose heartbreak does not even figure in accounts of the human rights violations of 1980.

But there is one person whose face we all know, whose face is the face of all our heartbreaks. A child standing in a courtroom. How old is he? According to his mother, seventeen, but according to the document forcibly extracted from the Institution of Forensic Medicine by the chief commander of the coup, Kenan Evren, "his bone age is eighteen". Erdal Eren, whose "bone age" was increased by the 1980 coup so he could be hanged, is one of the fifty people executed in the coup. Children are being herded in through the gates of Hell opened by the hangings of Deniz Gezmiş, Hüseyin İnan and Yusuf Aslan.

It's said that Erdal Eren killed a soldier, but the only visible evidence against him was that he had scratched the initials of an illegal organisation onto a wooden desk in his classroom. Erdal Eren provides one of the bloodiest manifestations of the boundless horror of the military coup. For the second

bloodiest, we must go to another city. In another city, we must examine a photograph that, at first sight, does not seem in the least bit bloody.

12. Joe the lovable dog and Turkish language lessons

What does it say on the door?

"One who repents from sin is like one who is without sin."
Prophet Muhammad

These words were written on the door of the prison erected in Diyarbakır, the epicentre of the Kurdish region. By all appearances associated with secularism, the coup presented religious solidarity as the country's uniting power rather than as a double nationality, as the AKP administration would say years later. Yet Esat Oktay Yıldıran, the infamous commander of the doubly infamous Diyarbakır Prison, which was filled to capacity on account of the coup, would shout at the leftist Kurdish prisoners in the courtyard:

"Allah is not here! *I* am here!"

Inscriptions on the truncheons, the most pervasive weapon of torture, supported him further:

"Allah is not in; the prophet is on vacation!"

Another resident of Diyarbakır Prison, which would come to be known as the Auschwitz of the coup, was Yıldıran's shepherd dog, Joe. Not only were the prisoners obliged to call the dog "commander", but families coming to visit prisoners also had to defer to him. Joe became a familiar face in Turkish political history, and the seeds of the Kurdish armed movement PKK were sown in the unimaginable torture chambers of this horrific prison. Before going on to make its mark on the 1980s

and then the 1990s, the PKK announced its formation to the whole nation with a bloody attack in 1984. The Kurds who refused to speak under torture now spoke, but not in Turkish. For this was written in the visiting area of the prison where they were subjected to torture for years: "Speak Turkish, speak more." Knowing no other language than Kurdish, the mothers of prisoners couldn't even utter endearments to their children whom they saw in the visiting booths in bloodied shirts. A sadly comic story of the time was the arrest of Musa Arter, famed Kurdish writer and thinker, on the grounds of "whistling in Kurdish".

* * *

For the curious:

Diyarbakır Prison Commander Esat Oktay Yıldıran started at a voice whispering into his ear one day in 1988:

"The man you tortured to death, Laz Ismail, sends his regards!"

A single bullet was fired point blank into his head …

The stage was set for the bloody 1990s.

Hold on a second, though! Can't we have a bit of fun?

13. Two moustachioed men

One of the moustaches is overweight and in shorts. Turgut Özal greets soldiers, his summery shorts belying his status as Prime Minister, installed by the coup. This indicates that we are now free. It's time to have some fun!

The rural-to-urban migration that began in the 1950s spawned *Arabesk*, a fusion of urban and rural cultures underscored by Arabic-inspired melodies. Although until the 1980s *Arabesk* songs had been about sweet self-pity and embracing poverty, now Ibrahim Tatlıses, the man in the second "moustache" photo, was caterwauling:

"I want some of that!"

After all, the "scholars and intellectuals" of the people are in prison, Prime Minister Özal waves the flag of the free market economy all over the country, and moral boundaries of 70's no longer apply. A phrase that first makes its appearance in comic strips becomes prevalent in all of social life:

"I may be a hick, but *I* have the money!"

Everything the previous generation had considered vulgar, the Prime Minister praises and endorses to the people. In

the publicity video for the Second Bosphorus Bridge he has constructed, he is seen crossing the bridge in a Mercedes with his wife, saying:

"Why don't you pop in a tape, Semra, and let's enjoy ourselves!"

As Turkey is demilitarised through the wearing of shorts, prisoners in military prisons still give their lives in hunger strikes against being forced to recite the National Anthem every morning, have their heads shaved and wear uniforms. The sounds of torture, however, are drowned out by the rise of Turkish pop music. The times are changing, and the words *vizyon* and *misyon* enter the Turkish language, never to leave again. Science becomes equated with technology, progress with the growth of capital, freedom with personal life choices, and happiness – more or less – with belly-dancing music.

14. The weeping child

When 1980 came around, a picture started to materialise in homes, cars and coffee houses everywhere. A little weeping boy. The whole country had become obsessively attached to this picture. Attempting to uncover the enigma of this mental state, the academic Murat Belge wrote in 1980:

What does the picture represent?

The first answer that comes to mind is that the boy is an orphan. In Turkey orphans are always pitied; the orphan is an established archetype of folk culture.

* * *

Turkey folk are folk who feel guilt towards their children. Our people have a paradoxical attitude towards children. On the one hand, we love them. People love the abstract concept of a child … oddly enough; everyone in our society loves other people's children.

We feel concrete love for a child only towards other people's children, whereas our love for our own child is abstract. Our society is one that is full of blame towards its children.

If a child who has no one but could belong to anyone (a child that recalls the neighbour's child rather than our own) is standing there with tears in his eyes, it could awaken sentiments dozing deep in the repositories of our conscience towards children. It's only natural that this child is popular, whom we bring home as a proxy for forgiving our crimes without blaming ourselves outright, who sentimentally wrings unprompted tears from us that we gloss over with phrases like "it happens, it's only human".

Throughout the 1970s, when children were dying in the streets every day, until the days of the coup, when youths were dying in prisons every day, the poster child spread until almost every lower middle-class household in the country had a copy. The reality behind the picture, however, was not really all that "sentimental".

In the 1970s in Izmir there was an imam who was begin-ning to win over the first of his devoted following: Fethullah Gülen. As the coup of 1980 drew near and the country slowly smouldered from the inside out, he preached this message to his followers:

"Don't ask questions. Don't rise up. Those who ask too many questions become instruments of the Devil."

He was on the side of equanimity and claimed that people should not venture into politics. In his opinion, rather than being swept up in the times' tempest, a new generation must be brought up. Acclaimed boys' summer camps were established in the late 1970s for religious and sports education, and, by the time the 1980s came around, they were producing docile and self-preserving followers in line with the Gülen Community's culture. The coup that put obligatory religious classes onto the curriculum, as well as Kenan Evren's religious references in every speech he gave, was appreciated by the community. The Gülen Community's periodical *Sızıntı* thus began publishing articles praising the "pashas":

"If the military had not come in time, we as a people would have had no recourse but to shed tears of calamity!"

Our little weeping boy, then, was the first cover of *Sızıntı*. The main article illustrated by the boy's image on the cover claims that the next generation must be "saved". A new "golden generation" is to be cultivated, an educated generation with fundamentalist and missionary leanings. The result is that this community – or "movement", as they call themselves – has been supported by every right-wing administration since the 1980 coup and has become a supranational economic, social and political force today. The AKP administration has been dependent on the intellectual, economic and political accumulations and international relations of the "golden generation" to remain standing. We'll mention in passing that, from the coup until the present day, the financial structure of the Gülen Community has never been monitored.

The weeping child of the 1980s has grown into a stern middle-aged man roaming the hallways of government. Who can tell? Maybe the statement that the Chilean Mediums Association made in 2008 was right after all: this painting, produced by an Italian artist, really was cursed!

15. The plastic prayer rug and Mekap shoes

I am talking to owners of small and middle-scale businesses from central Anatolia. Like others who were behind the boom in the economy in Asia Minor, they too are known as the Anatolian Tigers. It's the early 1990s and Turkey, as usual, is in disarray. But their faces are peaceful and their eyes gaze resolutely into a radiant future. After visiting dozens of such offices, I come to realise that their very expensive bookcases are invariably full of *Encyclopaedia Britannicas* with plastic prayer rugs on the top shelf, the kind the community uses when they overflow the mosque. Of the cheapest kind! The tackiest! The interesting thing is that these prayer rugs are always on top of the bookcases. Why put those prayer rugs up there, completely undermining the swank and ambience of the office? After asking each of them the same question, a question that was circumvented with the same sarcastic grins, one of them finally answers:

"No one in this country will do business with you unless that prayer rug is there!"

The verdict that "it has become impossible for those excluded from the community to survive economically in Turkey", which scientists and sociologists arrived at years later, was already clear as day to anyone travelling through Anatolia in the 1990s. It wasn't enough to merely be pious: it had to be visible to others, to the masses. That was the reason why the 1990s saw an unprecedented development in Turkey whereby mosques made sure that their communities "overflowed" in such a way as to disrupt pedestrian activity outside. When this "overflowing", being "so crowded that people couldn't fit into the mosque", finally came to be a political and economic force, the conflict between secularism and Islamic conservatism in Turkey began to overshadow all other conflicts. All other conflicts?

Say you sat down to dinner and turned on the TV to check the news. Dead lie on the ground. They wear salwars and some

dirty yellow variety of sneakers. They are "terrorists"! Invariably, they were "captured dead" after being hunted down in their "caves"! Seeing as they live in caves and are captured dead, they're surely not human. You don't have to feel sorry for them; you may go on eating. My generation is accustomed to starting dinner along with these visuals. Members of the Kurdish political movement that started mobilising in the 1980s were constantly being captured dead for "setting their sights on our state's unity and integrity". None of them had names or faces but, for some reason, they all had sneakers made by the brand Mekap.

We in the West never learned these names that the Kurds eulogised and idolised. Just like the Anatolian Tigers with the picture of the weeping boy in their homes, who showed off their plastic prayer rugs to one another, they too grew and grew and grew during the 1990s on the periphery of Turkey's collective attention.

16. Red carnations, chalk, a reef, pebbles, a Mercedes and a whistle

I don't much like red carnations. I doubt many in Turkey do. Yet red carnations were probably the most often sold flowers in Turkey during the 1990s. For the red carnation is the flower of choice in the mass funeral services held in the wake of political assassinations. We have good reason to be unnerved by the sight of this flower.

The 1990s will always be remembered for these mass funeral services. Not only were journalists, scientists and secularist figures in society all killed during this period, but thirty-seven intellectuals gathered in Sivas for a festival were also burned alive in a hotel by religious extremists. The most popular slogan chanted by the crowds in the funeral processions those days was: "The Mullahs to Iran!" Yet not only did the "mullahs" not go to Iran, they started to appear in the political arena as prominent and esteemed figures. Those who made a banner of the weeping boy picture, on the other hand, were probably only after the "religious education" of their own children at the time, because they didn't really concern themselves with the sixteen children who left their mark on the 1990s. Sixteen children who were detained for writing "free education" in chalk on a wall in Manisa were severely tortured, the cry of one of their mothers as they were taken away etched permanently into the country's memory:

"Don't take him! He's too young!"

While the light went out of lives because of a piece of chalk, Tansu Çiller, the pretty lady leader of the severely right-wing administration, acted every bit "like a man" and shouted:

"We'll more readily give our lives than a single pebble!"

In the midst of political turmoil and the customary chaos of the country, this lady became desperately consumed by a reef in the Aegean Sea, not unlike Margaret Thatcher's sudden and inexplicable preoccupation with the Falkland Islands! Just like Thatcher, she would become furious with the military and accuse them of "not being brave enough". In the grip of the same madness, journalists clambered from lifeboats onto the 400-metre-square reef and planted the Turkish flag, thereby hoping for relief from the madness induced by terror in the south-east. While the epic nationalist sermons and religious references in politics continued to become more and more widespread, those forced into prison by the coup were released in twos and threes. Emerging into a completely different Turkey, the leftist heroes of the 1970s were now in the 1990s perceived as caricature "losers" at best and withdrew into their own corners to the sound of their own sad music. Then, one night, among complaints that there was no effective opposition in the country, there was a car accident in the county of Susurluk, which, until then, had been known only for its *ayran*, which is basically diluted yogurt. The passengers of the Mercedes that collided with a truck were of great interest. A parliamentary member of the party in power, a police chief, and a fascist ex-militant with a fake ID.

So for weeks in every city of Turkey, people began blowing whistles, starting at exactly 9 pm. Flicking their lights on and off at the same time, they demanded full disclosure and an investigation into the "state–politics–mafia" relationship. That never

happened, needless to say. The Prime Minister, a handsome lady, would start to shout as soon as she was cornered:

"It is honourable to both fire and take bullets for the state!"

It should come as no surprise that it was around this time that the farewell ceremonies of young men leaving for their military service started turning into hysterical rituals. The country is in a state of mobilisation against "separatist Kurds". It is forbidden to call this a war: you must say "high intensive conflict" instead! It is dangerous to pronounce the abbreviation PKK as peh-keh-keh as the Kurds do. Speaking or singing in Kurdish might cost you your life, just as it would be a serious problem if flowers coincidentally bloomed in green, red and yellow, the colours of the PKK flag. It's as though this civil war has muted all the conflicts of society with the push of a button. The great "separation paranoia" has pushed all other political clashes into the background. Dozens of youths lose their lives in the hunger strikes that are started to protest against the building of single cell prisons. Vietnam syndrome, which will go on to define societal life in the years that follow, is talked about as little then as it is today. Youths returning from their mandatory military service seem "a little off", but when they try to explain, they are told in no uncertain terms that "there isn't a war in Turkey"! The first instances of the femicide that still shakes Turkey to the core today also started appearing during these years.

But there is also another Turkey. And the most discussed subject at the centre of this Turkey is love! Everyone is talking about the "boom in pop music". The "entertainment-seeking society" or the "generation of indifference" takes over 1990s' Turkey with all its might. Privately owned TV stations broadcast one frivolous programme after another and the country's ethical code, which has always frowned upon "being full when someone else is hungry", changes radically. The moral values of modesty, sharing, making do, austerity and solidarity are no more; instead, they are replaced by their polar opposites. An advertising jingle for cream cheese circulates on TV in the 1990s like an anthem for this frame of mind:

"Slap it on thick! Eat it quick!"

Right around then, on 28 February 1997, military tanks begin pounding the asphalt in Sincan, a district of the capital city Ankara. It's obvious why: a "tuning adjustment" has to be made to an Islamic conservative administration that appears to have renounced its secular orientation. Due to go down in history as the "post-modern coup", 28 February creates the circumstances of a coup without actually carrying one out. For this is the current political and social picture.

The momentous car accident known as the Susurluk incident has occurred and, since the passengers of the Mercedes that collided with the truck represent the state–mafia–politics triangle, the people are demanding the exposure of this type of shady collaboration. People turn their lights on and off every evening at 9 pm and the Islamist Prime Minister in power, Necmettin Erbakan, mocks the protests, unwisely disregarding the fact that the lights are going on and off in military lodges as well.

Turkey encounters the Ajzemendees, a radical Islamist sect, for the first time. With their head wraps and frocks, they appear first on the streets, then rapidly on TV, screaming: "We want sharia!"

Prime Minister Erbakan gives dinners at his residence for sect leaders and sheiks. This is especially jarring because the Prime Minister's residence is one of the symbols of the secular Republic. On consecutive days, these people designated as religious leaders – which, by law, is prohibited in the Republic of Turkey – are on the front pages of all the newspapers. In the past, the higher echelons of Turkish politics had collaborated with the leaders of religious communities, even the most reactionary ones, but to entertain them in the heart of the capital! That's unheard of.

In January 1997, high-ranking officers have a meeting in which they determine that "reactionism" is the greatest threat of all.

A heavy-handed theatre play performed at the end of January in the municipality of Sincan, a district of Ankara, is the rupturing point. The utterly outlandish play is full of jihadist propaganda and one of the guests is the Iranian ambassador. That is why, on 28 February, tanks set out for Sincan.

* * *

28 February 1997 instantly tipped the social and political scales. The rising figures of political Islam were forced to step off the stage. Some were apprehended, and lawsuits were set in motion. The prohibition of headscarf-wearing students from entering university grounds was the most visible aspect of this social and political tension. Demonstrations began to take place at universities. A closure suit was brought against Refah Parti, the Islamist conservative party in power. Prime Minister Erbakan resigned. The social democrat party formed a coalition with right-wing conservative parties. Pressure was put on the political Islamist faction on both the judicial and political fronts. No one knew in those days that the pressure this course of events put on the political Islamists would feed into resentment, leading to a policy of never-ending vendetta years later.

In the days that led to the post-modern coup of 28 February, standing in front of a crowd in a remote Anatolian city on 6 December 1997, a tall and passionate young Islamist politician began loudly reciting a poem that would change the course of history in Turkey forever. The country was as yet oblivious to all that it would have to endure ...

17. Big Brother Edi, Versace Islamo-Turkish flag

Edi might officially be the only Christian loved by hundreds of thousands of people in Turkey. The first champion of one of the first reality shows, a genre that was all the rage as our country entered the millennium, *Biri Bizi Gözetliyor* – Turkey's answer to *Big Brother*. Belligerent, an avid supporter of the football club Fenerbahçe, tall. Inarguably the most controversial character of 2001. For we have all started keeping watch of one another's privacy. We zap back and forth between live broadcasts of wars and real-time real lives. Meanwhile, today is the day when another belligerent, tall fan of Fenerbahçe is released from prison. He has served ten months for reading a poem to the crowds in a remote city in Anatolia, and in the interim he has turned into a political hero. The light bulb he has chosen as the symbol for his party is mocked. At the polls, no one gives him the time of day. For no one, as yet, is familiar with the name Recep Tayyip Erdoğan. But several years later, he will become so entrenched in history that posters reading "Objective 2023!" will be printed while Edi, whom we watch for nights on end, will fade into total obscurity. Prime Minister Recep Tayyip Erdoğan – the "tall man", "chief", "boss" – is representative of the Anatolian Tigers of years ago with their cheap plastic prayer rugs. He's a force of nature. He talks about democracy, knocks down the taboos surrounding the Kurds, broaches the subject of the Alevis, and, most importantly, claims that he will end the influence of the military over

political matters. Talking non-stop, he keeps making subtle references to his victimhood over having read a poem.

Those oblivious to the fact that the most acclaimed poets of Turkey served years in prison or died at night in suspicious circumstances cry over what this man was put through over a poem, embracing him deeply. He hates it when people say "moderate Islam"; he replies, "There is no moderation in Islam." The economic growth during his premiership, not that anyone can explain it, is so dazzling, his words about democracy so sweet that no one mentions the poem anymore. The poem, however, doesn't mince its words about what he means to do in later years:

> The minarets are bayonets, the domes our helmets,
> The mosque is our barracks; the believers, infantrymen.
> This divine army awaits my faith,
> Allahu Akbar, Allahu Akbar.

* * *

As soon as the secular factions in Turkey start growing apprehensive about all this, flags are grabbed and squares jostled into. These "Republic rallies" are denigrated as obsolete, pro-military and pro-coup demonstrations, their attendants mocked. At any rate, the organisers of these demonstrations are shoved into gigantic prisons built just for them in gigantic lawsuits that have hundreds of defendants. Such a political and social hegemony has been formed after ten years in power with an opposition that can only grab at straws, while large-scale corruption, mass worker deaths, ignominious encounters in international politics, and everything else imaginable is turned to the administration's favour – to the dismay of dissidents. While criticism is effectively rendered impossible, shopkeepers, greengrocers and other utterly ordinary people start believing that their phones are being tapped. Society is definitively cleaved between supporters and dissidents of AKP. The divide forged by the government is irreversibly deepened. Capital changes hands and Anatolian Tigers move into villas overlooking the Bosphorus in Istanbul, while a palace starts being built for Erdoğan in the Atatürk Forest Farm and Zoo in Ankara. The Islamic crowd celebrates this social and political victory with Versace headscarves and state-of-the-art automobiles. A pro-AKP businessman gleefully makes this declaration in the papers:

"You wouldn't see these brands of shoes in front of mosques in the old days. Now I'm seeing Gucci, Armani. It's wonderful."

One day, as AKP and Erdoğan hurtle towards a one-man regime, it's announced that three trees need to be cut down for the new configuration of Taksim Square. The scales of history are unexpectedly tipped once again as the country rises up in defence of those three trees. Which brings us to the present …

Since we are nearing the end of the photo album, it's time to remind Mr Turkey of a certain promise he made. He was going to tell us how he "symbolically" solved these intense crises of Turkey with a snap of his fingers. With this reminder, Mr Turkey quickly pulls out another photograph from underneath the nameless heaps. Two children with shaved heads. Who are they? They are no one. Then what? Here is what …

* * *

They sit on the grassy island in the middle of a roundabout. Both are all of five, at most six. Rations spread on the grass, they are having a picnic. It's a singular kind of picnic. There's a piece of cake with a candle stuck in it, a box of matches – a birthday celebration. Along with his friend, who is about the same size as him, Ayvaz is celebrating his birthday on a traffic island. He's happy. They look at the cake Ayvaz bought for 1 lira as though beholding a miracle. Because of the wind, however, they finish up the entire box of matches and still fail to light the candle. Therefore, he cannot blow it out. But it's clear they're having a ball. So the party continues, candle or not … we watch the police surveillance footage at dinner as "heart-warming news", but it doesn't end there.

The big strong policemen see the munchkins on the surveillance cameras. Classy policemen, what can I say. They go to the island. First they light the candle. Ayvaz blows it out. The pair is a little taken aback, but not suspicious at all. They laugh and clap when the candle goes out. But then, naturally, it's the moment of truth and they're taken by the arms and put on a minibus. They will be taken home.

The adventure is interrupted but the story goes on.

The news says: "Birthday celebration thrown for Ayvaz." There's footage showing the front porch of Ayvaz's home, a table placed there, and an extravagant birthday cake, empha-sising all the drabness, poverty and destitution that surrounds it. Ayvaz is standing to attention in front of the cake! Head shaved. They've first gone and shaved his head. The state's birthday gift to Ayvaz. He is now a pint-sized soldier!

* * *

His friend from the island is also there, also stricken with state-imposed baldness. It's apparent that Ayvaz is receiving directions off-camera. Smile! You are to smile! Blow! You are to blow out the candle! Clap! You are to clap. On the gleeful stage set up by father state, the birthday unfolds satisfactorily. The news divulges that Ayvaz's family is staggeringly poor. Ayvaz appears to be smiling but is actually tense and bewildered. Children other than his friend enter the frame. They clearly don't know Ayvaz very well and only want to appear in the picture. For their voices ring out: "Happy birthday, *Ayaz!*"

Ayvaz looks at these children who call him Ayaz and sing for him, crowded around a table in the middle of a poverty-stricken district. He laughs because he knows he must. He is now only playing the part of Ayvaz. He mostly looks at the cameras. He no longer exchanges looks with his friend. Neither of them seem to be children. Neither one seems to be himself. Their smiles seem unnecessarily forced. They are now on a stage set up through the collaborative efforts of the big strong policemen and the media. And very quickly – this can be observed with the naked eye – they learn to play-act.

Yet they were different as they clapped and excitedly tried to light the candle in the stupendous island birthday party of their very own construction. They had hair, for one thing. For another, they didn't look to anyone or observe themselves from the outside. They didn't mould their faces at the service of a camera and weren't as conscious of their poverty until their heads were shaved.

This is how the state solved the match-lighting problem at a private party for two children. It replaced the "civilian" cake with its own, their spontaneous smiles with uniform military greetings. You are to smile now, smile! You are to eat cake now, eat! Everything in a routine and sustainable artificiality. Allah keep our state from harm!

These bald children are the continuation of other bald children. The effort in Turkey to prevent differences, lest they pose a threat, through the production of monotypic people is a story that's been going on since the country was founded. Yet the country, too, was grabbed by the scruff of the neck, shaved, and made to stand to attention every time it tried to venture out from home to experience its own adventure, to mature, to create the entirety of a consciousness. For instance, it is possible to refer to the coup of 1980 – in whose shadow we still live – by this visual cue. Thousands of people were stuffed into prisons, shaved bald like Ayvaz, put through torture, made to wear uniform clothing and march up and down all day long like soldiers. Outside the prisons it's no different. This is also the reason why, until very recently, nearly all men had the same haircut. The coup distributed the prototype of the government worker hairstyle to every barber in the country, rendering them unable to cut hair in any other style and turning all men in the land into Ayvaz. It's important to point out that this attitude cannot be attributed solely to the military or to the state. The army is military, but civilians can't really be said to be civilian. Most of them have been duped in the same way Ayvaz was, acclimatising their bodies and souls to standing to attention from an early age. Since the inside of people's heads can't be tampered with, political crises in Turkey are solved by homologising the outside.

Women aren't exempt from all this. Let me give an example …

"Ms Unakıtan's headscarf significantly evolved over the course of six months into a 'modern style'. Unakıtan, who makes an effort to colour-coordinate her turban to her casual outfits, also received full points on her new style from fashion designers. Designers have pointed out that Unakıtan's modern headscarf-wearing style is the 'new headscarf fashion'. Noted to be especially popular among the young, this way of wearing the headscarf makes it possible to make a bow over the nape, as it is attached in the back with a pin."

The words you have just read are from a headline article in a 2003 issue of *Hürriyet*, the most popular daily newspaper in Turkey and the paper that is considered to represent the state and the status quo. With the title "The Wife of the Practical Minister Figures It Out", the gleeful news item drew attention to Finance Minister Kemal Unakıtan's wife Ahsen *Hanım*'s "agreeable" style and praised its modernness, while fingers were wagged at cabinet wives who still covered their heads in the old style, chiding them for remaining old-fashioned. Declared to be the "exemplary student", Ahsen *Hanım*'s qualities that were those "of the Republican woman", such as playing the piano and tennis, were emphasised and itemised. The writer went as far as to publish "before and after" photos of her in the context of "Look how well she has adapted to 'us'!" in order to applaud the modernism of her improved head-covering style.

Realising it wouldn't be rid of the business of conservatism any time soon, secular Turkey was endeavouring to identify and exemplify "headscarf-wearers who were sufficiently modern".

* * *

But what concerns us above all is the logo that was placed over the news story: "Let there be peace!" That is to say, how lovely it would be if the clash of modernism versus anti-modernism, if the two sparring sides with an antagonistic history behind them, could just make peace with "a bow over the nape". What the news item heralds is this:

"It would solve everything if you just covered your head like this instead of like that!"

There's an expression in Turkey, though I don't know if it's used in any other cultures for anything other than children's arguments:

"Kiss and make up!"

This state of false reconciliation or compromise is implemented after every crisis – Turkey has always "kissed and made up" since its founding, without actually solving a single one of those crises. For instance, militants of opposing political camps who killed each other prior to 12 September were put in the same cells under the practice of "mixing and conciliation". This was followed by news in the papers about "how well they get along!" Just like the issue of the headscarf solved by tying a bow. Just like the heads that are expected to become the same when they are shaved. Or, as mentioned at the very beginning, the "symbolic trial for the coup". Crises, however, keep on smouldering in the depths. Nothing has changed. Those who executed twenty-somethings on 12 March 1971 and those who executed a sixteen-year-old on 12 September 1980 are the same ones who wounded fourteen-year-old Berkin Elvan in the head with a tear gas canister and then declared him a terrorist as he lay on his deathbed in 2013.

I think we've seen enough photos. Let's close this album and get to the "fun" part – the present.

TODAY/
MORNING

"Geography, what do you want from me?"
– Graffiti, 2015

"Welcome to the land of the stimulus addicts! This is elsewhere, and not the world itself!" **– Engin Geçtan, Professor of Psychiatry,** *Life,* **2002**

"İdare et!"

Could it be a coincidence that, in Turkish, the word for "managing" and the word for "letting things slide" are one and the same? Or could it be that, over time, as the act of managing became tantamount to letting things slide, this turn of phrase came to describe both acts? And why must I go through the nightmare of arrest for the third time? My journals read aloud in court every time. Shame and fury … at the very least I don't think I'm paranoid anymore. Or it's knowing that, for the past couple of years, such nightmares have been beleaguering almost everyone. If it's paranoia, then it's collective. In the mornings, my friends and I relay our "courtroom memories" to one another and giggle over them.

"Today" I woke up with all this on my mind and implemented the only regimen I know of that can help me rid myself of such inextricable worries: going for a run! I've been running ever since the novelist Haruki Murakami wrote that, since writing novels is such an unhealthy occupation, it's necessary for novelists to lead healthy lives, to go for runs. I have yet to see any physical improvement, such as a dramatic increase in my book sales, but it's amusing enough just to irritate my friends, almost all of whom are depressed enough already due to the state of the nation. Where I run is on the European side of the Bosphorus, on the shore between the districts of Ortaköy and Bebek. The road inclines from the middle class to the upper. This is a road on which *kokoreç* and doner kebab shops eventually give way to steak houses, fishing boats to luxury yachts, traditional coffee houses to seaside "lounges". So there is no problem with me wearing the leggings I bought for running. One thinks of such things without realising. I wonder how a woman's psychological health is affected by the thought or the smidgen of anxiety lurking in her head, even if only subconsciously, that something might happen to her if she wears leggings? Or her intellectual capacity, for that matter? If a woman in Turkey were to try to make an inventory of the things she unconsciously worries about, calculates and mulls over on a daily basis, the list would probably be as endless as the numbers stretching to the right of the number pi. Hearing this might cause a Westerner whose experience with Turkey is limited to bathing suit and bikini-clad vacations to take us for paranoid lunatics. We have good reason for our paranoid delusions, however. For we've heard the story of a young woman named Didem Yaylalı. Epitomising present-day Turkey and the lives of many women, at first this story might seem to contain too many details. But trust me, this brief story encompasses quite a few of Turkey's issues.

A WOMAN'S "UNINDICTABLE" MURDER

"She was only a sweet, charming girl! It's only that she didn't live the way they wanted her to."

So claimed Evrim, best friend of Didem Yaylalı, who committed suicide in 2013, as she wept on the phone.

The young prospective judge had been found in a hotel room having taken her own life. The cause of death of the red-haired, cheerful future judge was disclosed as "leggings". Although she had completed all the prerequisites to start in her profession, the High Council of Judges and Prosecutors just would not make the decision to appoint her. But, naturally, this is not all there is to "a woman's unindictable murder". Let us read the story as it was told in the letter sent to me by Evrim, an engineer and Didem's roommate, the one who wept on the phone:

I would like to recount to you the murder of Didem Yaylalı, which was professionally orchestrated to drive her to suicide. Up until last year, when she found out she would never become a judge, Didem had been a very happy, vivacious and competent legal professional who worshipped the practice of law and knew by heart and kept track of every changing piece of legislation. From the moment she found out that she had not been appointed, Didem was consciously and deliberately thrust into a Kafkaesque world. She was neither fired nor appointed. In a hazy world, they worked at blurring her sense of what she was fighting against and how. Every time she hopefully knocked on their door, our very esteemed (!) judges at the High Council of Judges and Prosecutors told her, however indirectly, that she must abandon her principles and kiss their hands, or she would not be appointed.

One day when I got home from work, she asked me, "Evrim, what does conservative mean?" When I replied,

"It means to be reactionary, Didem, why do you ask?," she said, "A judge at the HCJP told me that that's how I have to be, that this is why such things keep happening to me." During her final months, in a bid to salvage her honour, Didem had been planning to work for just one day as a judge before resigning, in the event she was appointed. They would not even allow her to do this. They left Didem in purgatory. She was not even allowed to work as a lawyer.

She had plans that, as soon as she was let go, she would start interning as a lawyer. Since they would not let her go, however, she couldn't move. They tied her up and left her immobile. They consciously and willingly thrust Didem into a dead end. She had another friend, Nebi, whose dismissal on other grounds was then on the table. Nebi was dismissed last month, but no statement was ever made concerning Didem. Eagerly awaiting the dates on which the results were to be made public, Didem returned home in disappointment each time. If she was indeed at fault, why was she not being dismissed? They knew that dismissing Didem would mean rewarding her.

Only two of her friends from her class attended her funeral. Her friends (judges and prosecutors who had been appointed) did not, because they were afraid. They all knew about Didem's – legitimate – side of the story but wanted to secure their own futures. In a scaremongering, conservative society, voices such as Didem's, which rightfully clamoured for their freedoms, were muted. Didem had had many friends from her own class and those above her, prospective judges and prosecutors. They all drank and constantly said, "Just make sure no one sees or hears about it." Didem was unable to be so duplicitous.

Because they left Didem with no other option but suicide, because they deliberately killed a competent legal professional like Didem, because they have removed the word "freedom" from their lexicon, we know who they are and that they are guilty.

Tolga Onur, a friend of Didem's and another future judge who was not appointed due to not being "conservative" enough, has written the following, recounting the details of the Kafkaesque murder of a young and educated woman:

This is how the procedure goes: you are the subject of constant persecution, during which they do their best to find shortcomings. They want to find a rationale. The reason for that is to create an atmosphere of fear. You don't need to be on any one side. All they need is a piece of intelligence that you are not on theirs. So they go through Didem's files and find a report from months ago. She went to the hospital complaining of pneumonia. While the report had the hospital stamp and registry details, the doctor neglected to sign it. Just for this, they halted her advancement in rank as a punishment. In turn, the HCJP decided to "unappoint" her on the grounds of this punishment, just a week before she would have been appointed. A member of the HCJP apparently told her that she "must be conservative". When she was uncomprehending, they told her: "You need to be prudent. A judge doesn't go around in leggings." Didem was shocked because she only ever wore leggings at the weekend. Another member of the HCJP asked her: "Is there any chance you got pneumonia because you had been drinking? Are you having personal problems?"

In short, it is entirely possible to murder a woman with a pair of leggings and not leave a trace – you don't even have to strangle her with them either. Reported murders of women in Turkey have risen dramatically in the past decade. So much so that you might think that war has been declared on the women of Turkey. At least one such mind-bogglingly horrific murder takes place every day and rocks the nation to its core. But to commit such an invisible murder! That requires a small change in the Constitution. How?

In 2010, Turkey moved towards an amendment of the Constitution that came with the military coup of 1980. It sounded sweet to the ears: finally, "the Constitution overshadowed by the coup was going to change considerably". To be more accurate, that was how the amendment was presented to the masses by AKP. Although many changes had been made to the Constitution since 1982, AKP built its propaganda operations around the theme of "Turkey finally made democratic". The smidgen of truth in the propaganda was this: the coup leaders would finally go on trial. The act in the Constitution maintaining that the coup could not be prosecuted was being abolished. As you know from the previous chapter, no one was ever brought to trial, but this wave of giddiness was encouraged right up to the referendum. Tayyip Erdoğan,

Prime Minister at the time, worked his hardest for an amendment that all the other parties either opposed or were sceptical about. He even held one of his public rally crying sessions, which, as later research revealed, he unfailingly performed before each election. The worst part of it was that he cried over a subject that everyone in Turkey who had worked for justice, equality and freedom had also shed tears over.

Do you remember the name Erdal Eren from the previous chapter? From the lectern of the National Assembly, Erdoğan once again expertly confronted his dissidents with an ethical choice as he tearfully read the last letter of Erdal Eren, hanged at seventeen after his "bone age" assessment was tampered with, as well as the letters of the other prisoners who were hanged in the coup of 12 September. Did we not also want the perpetrators of the coup to be brought to trial, for the torturers to be exposed? We did. But in return we had to give Mr Erdoğan what he wanted. And what was that? We must allow him to change the composition of the Constitutional Court's members to favour the administration. We must also bar the Council of State from meddling with Erdoğan's affairs. Also, if possible, we must allow the administration to determine who joins the High Council of Judges and Prosecutors, which up till now had been autonomous. Meaning, if we would like to see Erdal Eren's killers in court, we would have to give him Didem Yaylalı. So we did. What occurred on the road to the referendum was a bit nauseating, to tell the truth. Those who claimed that this amendment would "compromise the division of powers principle" were accused of being "coup fanciers". Intellectuals were once again divided, as they had been since the day AKP came to power, yet much more sharply this time. There were those who smiled sardonically before accusing dissidents of being "coup fanciers", and those who scrambled in vain to explain to the oblivious public what the HCJP was and what the composition of this committee would entail. One slogan came to epitomise this period:

"Not enough, but yes!"

This meant: "Although this Constitution change falls short, we must still say yes." It was a discourse propagated by the highbrow liberals who lent intellectual validity to the administration. The administration on its own could never have passed the constitutional change by the public in regular circumstances, but it was approved in the referendum thanks to this brilliant method of propaganda. Didem Yaylalı wasn't the only one to die: soon enough, people pursuing their own lawsuits – political or otherwise – would openly advise one another at the courtroom entrance:

"If you're not one of them, they won't rule in your favour even if you're in the right."

Having had complete hold over the administration and legislation thanks to the Turkish electoral system, the party in power now had control over jurisdiction as well, the state's only remaining independent power. If you were to ask, as an outsider, "How on earth is that possible? How can you fool an entire country?", this is what led up to it all: *Gleichschaltung*!

And among intellectuals *Gleichschaltung* was the rule, so to speak. But not among the others. And I never forgot that. I left Germany dominated by the idea – of course somewhat exaggerated: Never again! I shall never again get involved in any kind of intellectual business. (Hannah Arendt, *Essays in Understanding, 1930–1954: Formation, Exile, and Totalitarianism*, 2005)

Gleichschaltung … for non-German speakers, it is impossible to even read at first, let alone enunciate. Yet it is a concept that, once defined, many people in Turkey would react to with, "Oh, right! *That* business!" Let me divulge the explanation made by the editor of the book cited above:

"Political coordination. A term that describes widespread surrender to the changing political climate of the Nazi era (in order to secure one's own position or find a job)."

Hannah Arendt, the political theorist and writer who witnessed the Nazi era, adds that the surrender in question is not made under duress imposed by the administration but completely willingly. It is this willingness that brought Arendt to the point of saying, "Damn all intellectuals straight to Hell!" It is the kind of willingness that anyone with a modicum of common sense who was close to the Istanbul intelligentsia during the past decade knows all too well. The literates who give oral reports no one asked for, the intellectuals who get in line without being commanded to, the "administration appraisal contests" that baffled even the powers that be. *Gleichschaltung* is a rather stale subject for us since the intellectual and political hegemony created by these "volunteers" was – thankfully! – eradicated by the Gezi protests. Stale, but still relevant.

My journalist friend Nick Ashdown, who works in Turkey, told me one day:

"Turkey's like a prison."

I thought he was going to talk about being oppressed, the violation of human rights or something of that sort. But what he said was something different:

"Just like in prison, you have to become a member of a political gang to save your life!"

Absolutely correct. There is, however, another important issue.

Those who've mingled with the Istanbul intelligentsia will know. There is actually only one major group. It is the gang of the Wholehearteds, those who are keen to ride whatever political or intellectual wave is currently trending. The Whole-hearteds gang has fought tooth and nail since AKP's first day in power to advertise the ruling class as harbingers of democracy. After the Gezi protests, they are no longer held in the same esteem. So much so that even Neil Faulkner, in the introduction to the Turkish edition of his book *A Marxist History of the World*, says:

"Turkey will not return to its pre-Taksim routine. A new age of protest has begun."

In the years before Gezi, however, when AKP was intellectually relevant as well as in power, as thousands were prosecuted and imprisoned unlawfully and in political trials, it was all very hazy. Many intellectuals, writers and journalists feared not the wrath of the ruling elite but excommunication from the intelligentsia. Being the spoilsport while everyone else is happily playing along is as fearsome to us as adults as it was when we were children. In this regard, what transpired when Çarşı, a group for fans of the Beşiktaş football club, was accused of a coup attempt due to its active role in the Gezi uprising proved to be very educational. Cem Yakışkan, store-keeper and spokesperson for the group, displayed a clarity and courage most intellectuals lacked.

Judge: You are being accused of trying to stage a coup. What do you have to say?

Cem Yakışkan: If we had that kind of power, we would make Beşiktaş win the championship!

Many intellectuals had been unable to answer with such clarity when journalists, union members, lawyers and students were accused through made-up evidence and ludicrous claims of trying to stage coups. The numbers of those eager to comply were tragically high. What's more, the foreign influx following AKP's rise to power could not be ignored. The international intelligentsia was so enthusiastic it was like it had been waiting for this day. In particular, it was the USA's designation of Turkey as a role model for Arab countries that won over many intel-lectuals. One of these was Slavoj Žižek. When Žižek claimed that Turkey could be a model for Arab countries at a time when hundreds of journalists, lawyers, students, politicians and union members had been imprisoned because of political persecution, I couldn't refrain from writing the following open letter:

Dear Mr Žižek,

As an attentive follower of your work, I feel obliged to write to you after hearing your comments on Turkey.

I share your admiration for my country, which I think made you say, "if the Arab world really needs a model, Turkey can be taken as a model". Yet I cannot help but repeat the sentence with which I concluded my contribution to the Doha debates on 12 January: "Turkey cannot be a model for the Arab world because it has enough problems already." One of the distasteful things about authoritarian regimes – as you might already know very well – is that they turn writers into imbeciles by forcing us to repeat the obvious over and over again. Such as: "Journalists should not be jailed"; "It is cruel to put Kurdish minors in jail"; "Tear gas shouldn't be used excessively, especially to a degree that causes death"; "Students holding a banner for free education shouldn't be put in jail for years"; "There should be no punishment without law"; etc. etc.

I have experienced an intimidating decrease in my own IQ lately, due to repeating the fact that Turkey is turning into a state of fear. Turkey's good people are already exhausted from running from one courtroom to another following political cases that could even inspire Kafka to revise his oeuvre.

That is why my dear friend, the journalist Ahmet Şık, when defending himself against a ridiculous indictment, quoted Roland Barthes saying: "Fascism does not only silence people but also forces them to speak." With another 103 journalists Ahmet has been jailed for about a year without any verdict. I invite you to admire the latest judiciary fashion of the season in Turkey: blurry accusations, no solid evidence but months or even years of detention. With more than 9,000 applications filed against it at the European Court of Human Rights (ECHR) in 2011, Turkey is the worst offender when it comes to freedom of speech. If those figures are not enough, you should know that a few days ago Ahmet's lawyer, during his defence statement, told the judges that prosecutors have been threatening him, arguing that his defence statement could result in prosecution under anti-terror laws. I think you would agree with me on his right to be alarmed, given that there are 40 lawyers in detention under that very anti-terror – thus anti-democratic – law.

I already know that you have no faith in Europe anymore so these figures might not interest you. Though I've heard that you are still inspired by Tahrir Square's call for freedom, I think our mutual friends in Egypt, Tunisia or Syria deserve better than our life in Turkey. Having lived in Beirut for a year, and covered the Tahrir stories and currently being based in Tunisia, I think that Turkey might even be inspired by some of those countries' appreciation for human life.

Because my compatriots who burn themselves to death have never been as legendary as Mouhammed Bouazizi of Tunisia. On 22 June 2010, the 20-year-old Erkan Gümüştaş set himself alight to protest the living conditions in prison. I am quite sure that only a few know his name in Turkey. His death hardly made it into the Turkish Human Rights Association reports, let alone setting the media ablaze.

Our police forces are no less merciless than the SCAF in Egypt. Metin Lokumcu, a teacher, died of a heart attack caused by the excessive use of tear gas during an assault on an anti-government protest on 31 May 2011. His friends were arrested under the anti-terrorism law when they wanted to protest against the violent crackdown on protesters.

The Kurdish children who, in order to earn some money, had to smuggle cigarettes across the mountainous border with Iraq have been no luckier than the young Syrian casualties. Their pictures didn't make it to the news when nine of them were killed after an "operation accident" in Uludere. The government decided to hush up the incident, and our Prime Minister stated that those who criticise the event are unfair towards the government. In the end, maybe Turkey simply has more shiny window dressing and better marks from the IMF for its economic adjustments. The last thing I want is to be one of those writers who have nothing to say about their countries except exposing the sins that are committed there. It is not only unfair to my country but also deeply hurtful for myself. Especially when you are doing it in another language, it bruises your emotional ties to your beloved country. I am sure you know what I mean. But it also hurts to see that you are serving the goals of an international marketing project by saying "Turkey can be a model for the Arab world". We, as people of Turkey, deserve better. As do the Arabs.

Yours,

Ece Temelkuran

* * *

Ultimately, the intelligentsia – both within the country and without – stamped Turkey with the "Bon pour l'Orient" pass, conceding that a mere handful of democracy would suffice for a country in the East. Such is the long story behind the death of Didem Yaylalı. The matter of not one of her friends coming to her funeral, however … now that is a little bit more complicated. It's better to tell you about that when we put on the notorious leggings and go for a run along the Bosphorus. The clean air of the Bosphorus might help clear your head after all that talk. The issue of "not being one of them" in particular … it would really help if you took a deep breath before I get into that fun topic.

"US" AND "THEM"

The shore of the Bosphorus is chock full of boats and, as the districts grow wealthier, yachts. Some of these yachts are currently set up as Ottoman palace boats. Or whatever it is that a tour company owner thinks of when he or she thinks of the Ottomans, or whatever it is that tourists desire when they come to Turkey from the Gulf after watching popular shows on Turkish channels. That means an excess of gilding, velvet and embroidery. Some boats even have Ottoman models (!) placed on their prows that could make even the most weather-beaten of us seasick. It apparently pleases tourists to have souvenir photos taken with display window dummies decked out in a moustache and beard and the attire of an Ottoman pasha. If you should grow weary of the "rediscovered past" nonsense along the shore, the inland side in turn is lined with billboards.

On the whole, the billboards fall into one of two categories. Either advertisements for shows or movies that are of a magnitude and frequency unprecedented in Turkey, soon coming out on national TV, or for "new life" projects. We'll get back to the adverts for shows and movies. The fact that descriptions such as "living space", "peaceful living" or "with people like you" are used to endorse construction projects with increasing frequency lays bare a glaring national truth: a nation's graffiti, public advertising and streets are its secret journal. Their codes have much to say to those who can decipher them and, as such, these advertisements can be quite closely related to the suicide of a young, healthy, middle-class prospective judge for "not being like them". The construction sector is the lifebuoy of underdeveloped economies – and, yes, that is one reason for the crazy multitudes of housing estates and apartment complexes. But the underlying message of "you must live with your own kind" in these advertisements is another issue entirely.

To understand, let us go back to the evening of 22 July 2007. AKP has won the election and the Prime Minister is about to give one of his famous balcony speeches. Ever since AKP came to power, the balcony speeches given the night of the election have come to be viewed as a democratic establishment, and the Prime Minister's declarations that night as prophecies higher than law. The nation's agenda is more dependent on what Mr Erdoğan has to say that night than on the activities of the party. On this night, marking AKP's second term in power, Prime Minister Tayyip steps out onto the balcony amidst screaming, the singing of marches and the general giddiness of a crazed crowd. The fun thus begins.

The Prime Minister addresses the crowd:

"Let me see those flags. What makes a flag a flag is the blood that is on it. Now let us from here say to all of Turkey: one nation, one flag, one homeland, one state!"

The Prime Minister might not be aware of it, but in the original the rest goes:

"*Ein stad, ein folk, ein Führer!*"

* * *

The slogan of those who let live only those who are like them, and annihilate those who are not. Further considering Mr Erdoğan's prompt "Objective 2023!", coming from the mouth of the leader of a party whose ethos is Islamist conservatism … you can imagine the rest.

* * *

After describing voters of parties other than AKP as "contributing to our richness" and proclaiming the half of the country that isn't pro-AKP to be "the nation's side dish", Mr Erdoğan continues:

"AKP is now the centre point of society!"

The following scene has been painstakingly composed to accompany these words at the very instant he utters them:

Mr Erdoğan, his headscarf-wearing wife Emine *Hanım*, Abdullah Gül and his headscarf-wearing wife Hayrünnisa *Hanım*.

Meaning that this is now the "median", what is "normal". Meaning that, if you don't look like them, you are now

143

marginal. Meaning that neither this state nor this people nor this public is yours; you are "other". At best you are a side dish!

* * *

Following the night of the election, everyone making appearances on TV to comment talked of the same thing: social reconciliation!

Business circles, the media and politicians who aren't pro-AKP constantly maintain that AKP must reconcile with other social factions and parties. "We hope it will be so", "We wish," they say. It is really a call for mercy. They ask for the mercy of the ruling class. For you cannot pressure a leader who has such social might as to bring him almost half of the votes; you can only call for mercy. You can only pray that he does not annihilate those who are not like him. And only *Führers* are asked for mercy, as you know.

* * *

And that, in fact, is what happened. After the night of the election, AKP removed its mask of democracy and civility. Now, in the squares, the Prime Minister clearly asserted "we" and, prior to admonishing those not like him, hollered:

"THEY!"

Mr Erdoğan was the pioneer in the matter of "they". From the instant he began to endorse the division of "us" and "them", a nation that was already precarious in its culture of coexistence split right down the middle. The cleft was thought to be between secularism and anti-secularism. At least, that's how it was during AKP's first term in office. There were even blatant notices in the papers: "For a Western kind of life ..." And then there were the promises of the housing estates where religious conservatives would reside: "For a serene life ..."

"Serenity" was the password of the conservatives. It meant that "they" were what stood between the conservatives and their serenity. Their personal space, as a matter of fact, was being afflicted with an intense attack of Balkanisation. Whenever the Prime Minister got up to speak, he would chase this kind of rhetoric:

"**We** have been victimised. Crushed. Yet now, even though we are in power, we tolerate **them**."

There is this rather coarse Turkish proverb: if the Imam breaks wind, the congregation will go one step further. As it is so coarse, it is often toned down:

"If even the Imam behaves like this, what wouldn't the congregation do!"

The more their "imam" talks of tolerance and endurance, the more the party's staff – and, at their heels, the Good Soldiers Švejk, as well as the ordinary people comprising the capillaries of society – start to do everything in their power to try to push "them" to the outskirts of society, the wind of victimisation at their backs. Didem Yaylalı was one victim of this trajectory. Let us enlist the help of the academician Fethi Açıkel's article "The Pathology of Sacred Victimhood" to understand it:

The ideological victory of [sacred victimhood] lies in its ability to mobilise the negative energy of the masses ("little America", "Great Turkey", "the Turkish world from the Adriatic to the Great Wall" etc.) into a higher level of politics, to propagate the optimistic belief that societal negativity will find its solution in a greater cause. In its ability to postpone "dissident negative energy" stemming from societal despondency through the promise of a victory in the future ... in its capability of transforming dissident energy in favour of the great ideal to turn it into a vehicle of negative sublimation ... in mobilising the dispossessed multitudes around a semi-authoritative, semi-aggressive *telos* that they can internalise on a spiritual level and commanding the societal negative energy ...

Prior to his rise to power, and following it, the Prime Minister also kept mentioning a historical victimisation, the state of collective victimisation. "THEY," he would begin, "didn't take us seriously, they didn't let us exercise our faith, they held us back, they took away our rights, they scorned us, degraded us." As though Turkey had been ruled by a severe, anti-religion socialist regime since its founding, but finally "the masses would have their say!" The Prime Minister spoke of a "new Turkey", of the "great Turkey". And, just as in the article above, he postponed that bright day:

"Objective 2023!"

And at the same time as he impoverished already bereft masses through the most savage capitalist policies, he goaded them in the squares with these words:

"You are Turkey! Think big!"

So there it was: those who could see the "pathology" and refused to be a part of it, who couldn't live with this deceptive enthusiasm, were now also "they". If they couldn't adapt to "us", then they may as well be alone. Just like Didem Yaylalı … "We", on the other hand, were always the victims. Always. Even when charged with fraud with transcripts as proof, when hundreds of people were imprisoned on political charges, when no dissident voice could find an outlet in the media, when people were beaten to death for not fasting, when the Turkish lira plummeted against the dollar, or when 301 labourers died in a single night in a mine operated by government-affiliated capital, the government was "victimised and wronged" and it was all a conspiracy against them. Sacred victimhood always validated the "propensity for vengeful indemnity". So much so that the following transpired, which, looking back from now to 2012, reads like a black comedy.

* * *

You were the one who produced and distributed the bad milk, we heard. We decided to drop by and see who you are. Don't get us wrong, we don't think you are the only guilty party in this business. Those who fell for your moderate Islamic-style moustache and the scent of the rose oil that you wear – the ones who granted you the contract in this milk business – are the real guilty party.

It is natural that such a filthy government has such filthy milk.

You have nowhere to run to. Because now there is Redhack!

PS: We didn't really hack you. What you are seeing is only psychological!

147

This text was seen on the websites of three big milk companies. An anonymous, dissident hacker group that calls itself Redhack left its message on the web pages with a souvenir photograph. In the photo, all the group members were wearing grinning *V for Vendetta* masks.

Following the action, they were praised by many on social media platforms, some calling them "the Robin Hoods of Turkey". One might think that the title "Robin Hood" is excessive for only having hacked the web pages of three milk companies. Also, their message was not clear to people who did not know what was happening in Turkey then. Here is the story. When the school milk project began, the plan was to distribute free milk to millions of students in schools. Everything started quite cheerfully. For the first few hours of distribution, the little boxes of milk brought glory to the government.

Then news arrived from twelve different cities. As the hours went by, the news outlets had difficulty keeping up with the rising number of children who had been hospitalised with symptoms of food poisoning. When journalists wanted to confirm the bad news, some of the city mayors came up with a particularly interesting argument: "The kids are not poisoned. The whole thing is psychological." This, in turn, inspired Redhack to "psychologically" hack the websites.

By the end of the first day, 1,193 children had been hospitalised.

The following day, the media expected some statements on the issue to be released, at least something relating to the physical state of the children rather than their psychological condition. So, the government spokesman took the stage only to shock the media even more. He said: "It is not poisoning. It might be overdose, though. In certain situations, when milk is drunk for the first time, such cases might occur." Although it was only three sentences long, the content of the statement was rich enough to create a flood of bitter jokes and even more outrage.

Most people debated which was more outrageous: an authority announcing that kids "overdosed" on milk or revealing the fact that thousands of children in Turkey tasted milk for the first time in their lives in primary school. Similar statements were made by other ministers. Even "kids being too hungry" was given by the officials as a probable reason for hospitalisation. Since a certain amount of rage was expressed on social media – not in the mainstream press, of course – the political authority was quick to condemn the "unfair reaction" to their great project. The Minister for Nutrition, Agriculture and Livestock said that "the government will continue with the school milk project despite the provocations". After this statement, many on social media platforms were predicting that the government might interrogate the hospitalised kids for "plotting against the government by letting themselves be seriously poisoned".

Some said that actually there was nothing wrong with the milk but the children were not right, and therefore the kids should be checked and fixed, not the milk.

Then came the second day of the milk distribution project. One might expect that after such a reaction more care would be taken, but that was not the case. Starting in the morning, news started flowing. Hundreds of kids were in hospital.

It would be extremely unfair or partisan against Islam to claim that the government did this on purpose. But on the second day of the school milk campaign we learned that the government had recently been presented with a motion in Parliament concerning the regulations relating to the school milk project. The Republican People's Party had submitted a motion against the government concerning the standards that the government applied to those companies that were selling milk to the state. Unsurprisingly, it was not answered then and is still unanswered. None of the milk companies made any public statements either.

At his party's youth branch meeting, Prime Minister Erdoğan gave an extremely exciting speech to his young followers. One sentence of his was particularly memorable. He said: "I want a young generation who holds onto their religion! I want a youth who holds onto their grudge!" Clearly, he didn't want a new generation that is plotting against him by getting poisoned!

* * *

As a generation that "held onto their grudges" bloomed, the rift between "us" and "them" grew wider. The dividing line was not secular/non-secular but obedience. If it hadn't been, İhsan Eliaçık, translator of the Koran into Turkish and distinguished in Islamist circles, would not have been among the personae non gratae of the time. It was a movement born of fury and resentment, set in motion with the objective of taking over people's lives completely. When İhsan Eliaçık, together with several Islamist writers, organised the "Earthly

Suppers" against "greed and mercilessness" during the month of Ramadan, it was made clear that the divide had more to do with deference to the party than with religion. As Eliaçık broke his fast in the street with the homeless and other intellectuals, he chose as his locale the front porches of the five-star hotels where AKP supporters and members broke theirs, and so the AKP youth who "held onto their grudges and religion" could denounce the religious scholar as an infidel for criticising their party.

* * *

Let us conclude our increasingly stifling Mrs Dalloway jog with a few last words concerning the buildings illustrated on the aforementioned billboards. Not only are these buildings erected as monuments to the divide between "us" and "them", but they also rise as pointers to AKP's "New Turkey" project. For the present process in Turkey is not one of Islamisation but of Dubaisation.

* * *

The government in Turkey loves shopping malls. They don't love them merely as glittering indicators of a prosperous economy; they think opening new shopping malls is a magic solution for the most serious political and social problems of the country. During the last ten years of AKP governance, all of Anatolia has been filled up with mushrooming shopping malls. With their bling-bling building façades on the outside and constant, loud music in the inside, they are the sacred places of worship of capitalism, the beating heart of cities, but not only that. Like other shopping malls in other parts of the planet, they create a new stereotype. A person floating in between the shops. A breed not necessarily consuming but filling his or her time – their life itself, so to speak – contemplating consumption. Since the majority of society is incapable of consuming the goods available for sale in the shopping malls, they go there just to see other people consuming and to be "there", close to the warmth of prosperity. Youngsters especially, boys and girls from the cities' poor neighbourhoods, form groups to organise daily tourist visits to the glittering life of the upper class. The malls don't serve only as a new version of the Agora – in this "modern" version you cannot speak due to the volume of the music and the endless echo of the sounds – they also provide visitors with a certain feeling of security in a segregated community. As the streets get more conservative and less secure, the malls feel like a parallel universe where everything is more hygienic and less tense. They allow people to disguise themselves as the rich – including the shopping assistants, who are mostly on the minimum wage. With the freedom to consume or to live the illusion of consumption, people feel "free", as I was told once when I conducted interviews with the poor wanderers of the malls. A new human being is being created, silently in awe of the endless display of commodities and suffering from an addiction to bling. Just like in Dubai.

The AKP officials and the Prime Minister prefer to refer to the shopping malls as the sign of a prosperous country. If you are not a visitor to this parallel life, if you are not fine with freedom to consume or the illusion of consumption, then there really must be something wrong with you. This automatically means that you are excommunicated from "society" and become an outsider, which, as we are taught very well, means invisibility on a good day and tear gas on a not so good day. "Come to our very own Dubai," they say. "What more do you want, for God's sake?"

The Dubaisation of society is not a Turkish invention, obviously. The creation of parallel lives in conservative societies happens on a monumental scale in the Gulf countries. Now it is invading Turkey as well. At first sight, the government-supported mall invasion seems to be a product of limited societal projection. But when you take a closer look, it is actually a very well formed social project to reform the individual into a being, one who will carry on his shoulders the obedient consumption of a society with conservative values. It is a dream of being the "little Muslim China" for a country that was once expected to be a "little America".

Furthermore, Dubaisation was a project aimed at taking people out of public space and putting them inside buildings, in order to abolish the status of the streets as a political and social space. Therefore, it was no coincidence that the Gezi protests, which we'll get back to at length, were set off by trees being cut down for a shopping mall due to be built in Taksim. The Gezi uprising was a protest against this great social project that was to reshape not only the city but individual vision as well.

Since we're halfway along our running route, we'll talk about the billboards on the inland side of the road that show adverts for state-sponsored TV, and their connection to the suicide of Didem Yaylalı, before we finish in the district of Bebek. As it is, there is much more to do and talk about "today".

THE HOUR OF "LONG LIVE OUR PADISHAH!"

There are quite a few Ottomans on the billboards. Padishahs, pashas, young and brazen Ottoman thugs. All are well groomed, all gaze deeply as though possessed by some spiritual vision. The names of the shows, too, are odd: *Resurrection, Crux, The Conqueror* ... The posters also feature beautiful women praying and ugly women not praying. These are huge productions by state-owned television companies. It is obvious from their vulgarity and the crude clarity of the points they make that their purpose, rather than art or entertainment, is education. Just like the propaganda films made with the backing of the Ministry of Culture, they too receive the state's support in a way no ordinary film ever does. Their task is to psychologically prepare the public for "New Turkey". Every one of them defends the aesthetic of rural conservatism as opposed to the urban, middle-class and secular lifestyle. Speaking of which, let us talk about the mayor of Ankara, a world brand and all-round legend in this regard. He started as Ankara's mayor in 1994 and his first accomplishment was to demolish a statue on the grounds that its breasts were exposed. He went down in Turkey's history of aesthetics that very day with this aphorism:

"I spit on such 'art'!"

It's 2015 and he is still the mayor. Over the years, he gradually replaced the statues he demolished with new ones. As this book was being written, he added to his array of count-less oddities the endeavour of erecting a robot statue in the middle of the capital. Faced with loud protests, he made this statement:

"I'll have it removed and replaced with a dinosaur statue!"

He also has the singular passion of bedecking Ankara with clocks. It's the final link in his chain of achievements, such as erecting gigantic plastic statues of athletes all over the city, the cartoon characters installed at the city's entrance, a statue of a teapot, artificial waterfalls made out of plaster, underpasses tiled in a bath-house style, traffic lights that blink in cryptic patterns and confuse everyone, the direction of flow on the roads, which he changes nightly, and countless others. Allow me to add that some of the clocks are shaped like wristwatches. I feel that Ankara has enough of a "cabinet of curiosities" vibe to attract tourists. I've no doubt that the countless bizarre shenanigans of the mayor of Ankara would prove more entertaining for tourists than looking at "fairy chimney" rock formations. At the very least, such a tour could be a magnificent introduction to Turkey's nonsensical psycho-logical state.

The Time Regulation Institute is one of the great works of Turkish literature. Relating to the crisis of modernisation that occurred in Turkey as early as the 1950s, Ahmet Hamdi Tanpınar imagines an institution whose only function is to synchronise clocks:

"Being a realist does not mean seeing the truth for what it is. It is a question of determining our relationship to the truth in a way that is most beneficial for us."

155

Just like the mayor of Ankara, all the other members of AKP have, quite correctly, determined their "relationship to the truth" and have a perfect grasp on the "reality" that what matters is keeping the Prime Minister happy – or the "Chief", as they informally refer to him. Not much else matters; as long as they obey, they will be able to realise whatever weird fantasy occurs to them. Just like the pro-AKP crowd that gathered for the balcony speech following the elections of 30 March 2014 … they knew, just like Goebbels in his time, to synchronise their watches to the party in power:

"I have no conscience; the Führer is my conscience!"

Preceding the elections that day, which once again culminated in victory for AKP, Turkey had witnessed the deaths of two children. I'm going to leave aside the fact that enormous malpractices implicating the Prime Minister's family and friends were exposed right before the elections, somehow enabling AKP to craft another rhetoric of victimhood. On this night, the Prime Minister took to the balcony, together with his relatives and ministers who allegedly had taken part in the malpractices, to give his speech of victory. Let us leave aside the disgrace that they smugly embraced and return to the main issue of the two children.

Ece Su was five years old when she boarded a ferry in the car driven by her mother. The ferry pulled away just as they were boarding, and Ece Su drowned. Those who talked about the incident or called for attention on social media were flamed by pro-administration Twitter users.

"What is it you're after?," people speculated. "You're trying to provoke," they accused. There were even those who said, "She had leukaemia; she was going to die anyway." This happened to such an extent that people were deterred from even demanding the identification of those responsible for the death.

The next death, the whole world heard about.

Fourteen-year-old Berkin Elvan sustained a head injury from a gas capsule at the beginning of the Gezi protests and, after remaining in a coma for months, passed away at the age of fifteen. Millions of people from all over the country took to the streets with the demand, "We don't want any more child deaths. Stop the police violence wrought by the administration"; they were dealt their share of that violence.

His parents were not even allowed to mourn, as the Prime Minister prompted the crowd to boo Berkin's family during his pre-election rallies, accusing them of being terrorists.

These two deaths took place before the election. Then it was time for the election, which culminated in the Prime Minister's after-election balcony speech, which had become an institution in our democracy.

The Prime Minister's declarations were eerie. "We are at war with Syria," he suddenly blurted out.

Before we could be shocked by the fact that none of us knew this, he raced on, claiming that those who "conspired" against him would be "ambushed in their dens".

Even if not against Syria, the Prime Minister called for absolute mobilisation against his opposers. Supporters who had gathered for the victory speech followed up every declaration of hate with giddy slogans:

"Long live our Padishah!"

These were the days when the results of the elections remained murky and the accusations of malpractice were all too serious. Some of AKP's opposition had withdrawn into the cynical approach of "Let's not have any more elections; it's not worth the expense." Almost everyone now had a deep understanding of Stalin's claim: "It doesn't matter who votes. It matters who counts the votes."

In a system where jurisdiction had lost its reliability and impartiality, where the administration openly admitted to disregarding the law, and where legislative power was completely stymied by the rulers, the one conduit that remained beyond control was the street. That is, if you could withstand the tear gas.

On the other hand, AKP's militant supporters, who for a time had been relatively silent in the face of malpractice claims, once again went wild with courage when the Prime Minister claimed victory before the polling had even ended. It took them only two days to dominate both the street and social media with the mindset that anyone and anything that was unlike them would be destroyed.

The question "Is someone setting the stage for civil war?" – which, until then, had been a scattered and occasional rumination – began to be voiced with increasing intensity and frequency.

It was at this very point, as a dark cloud of desperation descended over Turkey, signalling the complete annihilation of conscience, morality, the justice system and any existing common ground, a piece of news showed up on Twitter that had nothing at all to do with politics. Three and a half-year-old Pamir had disappeared after his noon nap. The Twitter community adopted Pamir with an apprehension well beyond the normal. In fact, Turkey seemed to proclaim: "We cannot tolerate holding the funeral of another child."

Not too long afterwards, hundreds of people claiming to be AKP followers took to Twitter to cry conspiracy. Along with claims that the child was Alevi, and that Pamir would be used as fodder to provoke demonstrations, they worked to build up hatred towards Pamir and his family. The search party naturally retaliated in the face of the "limitless evil".

They repeated the question that Adorno and Freud and Arendt had once asked:

"How can they be so evil?"

It wasn't the corrupt elections or the allegations of electoral fraud directed at the administration, or the political trials aimed at eradicating individual opinion ... the question arose in the minds of not only intellectuals but also anyone else who kept track of political developments:

"Where will all the malevolence, hate, alienation and cheering for hostility end?"

The Prime Minister now branded as the "trash of society" those he had proclaimed to be the "side dish" of society seven years ago. And he demanded of his fervid, vindictive followers: "Do the best you can!" Everyone who witnessed the unrestrained fury of this devoted crowd with its cries of "Long live our Padishah!" came closer to knowing how best to synchronise their clocks. The TV channels, municipalities, journalists and the common man knew better than to ask "Padishah?", instead turning to their television sets to better understand the impending regime of the Sultan through the broadcast shows. Didem Yaylalı and her counterparts, on the other hand, stared at these clocks and these screens and asked, with the same pained bewilderment that has remained unchanged throughout the history of humanity:

"How can they be so evil?"

If you're not tired yet, it might help to dwell for a while on the following words: pained bewilderment. For this is something we all know only too well despite never having discussed it as much as we should have done.

The year: 1941.

The day: 22 June.

Ivan had never fought with anyone in his life

(not even with the good-hearted but very prickly
Armenian Sagamanian),

not because he was afraid
but because he loved peace.

And he harbored no ill will toward any nation.

Ivan had one weakness:

he was easily amazed, like a child.

And he was strangely pained and amazed

by Hitler's rise in Germany. Despite the Social Democrat's betrayal,

the nation of Marx and Engels, Beethoven and Schiller,
the proletariat, our Communist comrades, and Telman
will bring him down for sure,
Ivan thought.

Hitler was not brought down.
Ivan was more amazed, more pained.

(Nazım Hikmet, *Human Landscapes From My Country*,
translated from the Turkish by Randy Blasing and Mutlu
Konuk, 2002)

Many of us, throughout the history of humanity, have been
baffled by the same question, posed in a spectrum of languages,
and the pained bewilderment of this question will continue to
drive many of us mad, until our species ceases to exist:

"How can people not want to live in a more humane
system?"

This tiny and deeply, deeply humane question lies at the
heart of thousands of deaths and millions of bruised lives,
ranging from Sheikh Bedreddin to Marx, from Mustafa
Suphi, Turkey's first unsolved murder, to Berkin Elvan, who
died at fifteen because he was hit by a gas capsule fired by "an
unidentified police officer" during the Gezi protests. It seems
a childish inquiry:

"How can people choose oppression over resistance?"
Or this:

"How is it that people worship and serve their oppressors?"

Humanity expects from humanity beauty, righteous-ness, the most humane. Especially in the roughest of times. And yet ...

When people are faced with enough injustice and brutality, children start attacking humanity. Brutalised suffi-ciently through pain, injustice and cruelty, humanity is an organism capable of self-annihilation. To react to a blow as naturally as though one were an object, to show resistance as a natural reflex against oppression ... Oh! What a lovely dream it would be. Humane, supremely humane, and yet too lovely to be true.

Great responsibility falls upon those who were swept up by this dream. That means they have to convince people to chase a dream that has never been known to come true: we can create Heaven on earth! Throughout history, the most estimable members of the human race have been slaughtered because of this dream by the least estimable ones, who were convinced it was only a dream. Those who believed in their fellow human beings were almost always declared "enemies of the people" by those who worshipped power. This accusation has always been the greatest yet most easily believable lie in the world. And always they froze in pained bewilderment. Just like we have here in Turkey for the past ten years, at a loss for words as we angrily puzzle over how things can be the way they are. As with Didem Yaylalı ...

How was it that the Prime Minister remained powerful and unvanquished after all these child deaths and accusations of corruption? One of us who puzzled over the situation, Ozan Tüzün, made this discovery in 2013. You are free to examine the following excerpt if you too happen to have a figurehead who is driving you insane – you might find it beneficial. Tüzün has ruminated over Mr Erdoğan's methods and has figured out the algorithm that enables him to feign innocence despite all his crimes, and to convince the masses of his unparalleled victimhood despite all his power:

Tayyip Erdoğan has an algorithm he has perfected over the years that he resorts to in answering anything he is asked. As a communications graduate, I have attempted to examine it.

The algorithm is made up of several steps and, when given enough time, he will use them all (1 through 8), whereas if pressed for time, he will use only a few (in general, 1, 3 and 6).

I'll explain myself better through an example. I shall return to Erdoğan's childhood and presume he has broken a vase at home.

Tayyip is alone at home and his mother returns to find the vase broken.

Mother: Tayyip! Did you break the vase?

Step 1: Change the rhetoric around the wrongdoing in order to stop it from being wrong and try to portray it as something good.

- I did not break the vase, I merely dismantled it so it will be convenient to rearrange.

Real-life examples of this technique are:

- "We are not harming the trees, we're uprooting them to transport them."
- "I did not change, I improved."
- "We are not banning alcohol, we are regulating its use."

Step 2: Convince people that you are the last person on earth who would commit that offence or make that mistake.

- Why would I want to harm the vase? I'm also a vase. I am the vasiest vase there is. When that vase was bought, I was the one who carried it up four flights on my shoulder, and – I'm giving you the exact numbers here – *ninety-three steps,* up the stairs. I was the one who said we should put it in storage so it wouldn't fade in the sun. I was the one who, once again, covered it up when my friends came over so no one would get jealous and jinx it. I am the vase's number one supporter, so why on earth would I want to harm it?

Real-life examples of this technique are:

- "Why would we want to cut the trees when we have planted exactly 3 quadrillion of them?"
- "Why would we put pressure on jurisdiction when we are the ones who built the biggest courthouses in Turkey and gave them the greatest facilities known to the Republic?"

Step 3: Undermine the importance of the issue at hand, normalise it and proceed to explain through examples how things could have been much worse.

- Besides, I don't understand the big fuss over the rearranging of the vase. Vases are obsolete decorative objects mostly used in old communist countries. Do you see America or England having vases in *their* houses? Do you ever see them in the movies? In modern homes? At best, vases are baroque thingamajigs left over from Ceausescu's Romania or the oblasts of Ukraine that are still afflicted by socialism. Do they have any place in the modern world? No. It's impossible to make sense of your reaction. I personally think the rearrangement of the vase was a long time coming.

Real-life examples of this technique:
- "We're not the only ones with alcohol regulation. You think we came up with this? Just look at Scandinavian countries, at France and England, their regulations are hundreds of times tighter. The ones we have are entry level."

Step 4: Use affection and wisdom to crush your opponent. Claim you didn't do it when you could have.

- You come to me with these accusations when I could have broken that vase twenty times over. I'm home every day with the vase. Why didn't I break the vase before if you think I'm so hostile? I could have broken it, I could have even made it disappear forever, but I didn't. I didn't do it even though the vase and I don't see eye to eye on most things, because I respect your opinions. The people's right to love the vase is sacred to me. I love the vase not because it's a vase but because of its creator. I'm willing to vouch for every vase in this house.

Real-life examples of this technique:

• In truth, this is used not only by Erdoğan but also by his entire party. Current examples include: "We could have cut off the internet during the Gezi events, but we didn't." Or, to quote Melih Gökçek, "We could have strangled you then and there and democracy be damned."

Step 5: Never leave a question unanswered. Answer the question in the vein of: "Let's assume what you are saying is true." Accept the possibility and demonstrate your responsible attitude towards it.

• Let's assume what you say is true. What you say did indeed happen to the vase. Does that mean I'm to blame for everything? It could have been an air current or the cat that knocked it over. I've given the necessary instructions to Mustafa, the neighbour's boy, to investigate the matter. He will look into the speed at which the wind was blowing yesterday and examine the cat's behaviour and report back to me. If I detect any wrongdoing, I will personally punish the cat myself. I will fix the windows myself. I'm keeping an eye on everything. I'm doing it all for our home, for the beauty and well-being of our home.

Real-life examples of this technique:

- "There have been complaints about the overuse of tear gas during the Gezi events, it's true. I've given instructions to the necessary parties for these matters to be investigated. If this is indeed true, it will be investigated and dealt with accordingly. We will not and cannot allow such a thing to happen."

Step 6: If someone disputes your version of events, question their sincerity.

- There's also this point to consider. The vase in the living room is hardly the first vase in the world to have been rearranged. Seeing as you are so sensitive about vases, why didn't you react when the downstairs neighbour's vases were broken by their son, not once but twice? Where were you then? Why didn't you join in Auntie Ayşe's tears that time her china broke when she was moving? Is this vase special because of its relation to me? Your intention here is not to eat the grapes but to attack the grape grower. The vase is merely an excuse.

Real-life examples of this technique:

- "If you like trees so much, where were you when I was falling all over myself to prevent a university from being built in a forested area? Where were all these crowds then?"
- "If you're so crazy about freedom of the press, where were you during the 28 February era?"

Step 7: You are in the clear, having managed to talk your way out. Now use this to your advantage to undermine your opponents.

- This breaking the vase business, that's exactly the kind of stuff Ali (my little brother) would do. That's what he does. Who broke the pane of glass in the cabinet last year and kicked a ball at father's record player when he was little? Ali. Ali is the one with the vase-breaking mindset. He's behind this one as well, let me tell you. With the time for father to determine our allowances approaching and him not being able to beat me at school, he thinks he's found a way to get one up on me like this. Father is quite aware of all of this. He always makes fair decisions, so I've no reason to worry. I talk to my father all the time.

Real-life examples of this technique:

- "All these demonstrations and riots are products of the CHP [Republican People's Party] mindset. They're the ones behind this: with the elections approaching, they think they've found a way to get at us. They're organising the marginal factions, attempting to get a bunch of looters to kick up a fuss. We know our people better than that; our people are not easily fooled. The people see all."

Step 8: The matter has been concluded and answered for. Wrap up your speech to your advantage, boasting of your character and actions.

- None of this matters to me, mother. I mind my own business. Just look, in my two years of middle school, I've become top of my class. I get pointed out by everyone; the other kids' mothers tell their sons that they should be more like Tayyip. That's where we are. Perfect scores for religion, PE, maths. That's where we are. I mind my own business; I mind my lessons. I strive and will continue to strive to be a worthy son for my family and to elevate my family's status to being the most exemplary family in the building, as my father also says.

* * *

This communicational and political abracadabra or rhetorical algorithm does indeed exist. The motive behind "Long live my Padishah!", however, lies unfortunately not in words but in bread. Meaning that sovereignty is won first and foremost through people's stomachs rather than their brains.

Here is the quick version of people's schooling through hunger and lethargy.

After the suppression of mass humanitarian struggles through military coups in 1971 and 1980, the human rights struggles against paramilitary state forces in the 1990s, and the outcries over the poverty caused by the oppressive policies of the IMF, which bring us to the 2000s, only AKP gave bread and the promise of hope to the poor. The network set up by Fethullah Gülen's community united with the party's local organisations and "lent a helping hand to the poor" under the guise of welfare. The capital in question was of murky origins and votes were openly exchanged for a packet of burghul or flour or a bottle of oil. The general consensus of dissent in those days was that rights were being doled out as charity. A society dependent on such charity was slowly forming and, as in all other societies based on charity, everyone's fate depended on the mercy of the "giving hand". İhsan Eliaçık, one of the administration's least favourite people, would go on to claim: "According to my calculations, a minimum of 100,000 people's material and spiritual existence depend on the presence of Mr Erdoğan." In fact, the survival of millions of people depended on AKP staying in power. Hence, for the millions who had to believe in anything "the Chief" claimed in order to comfortably maintain their lives, the feckless abracadabra was not an issue. In a charity-dependent society, the idea of cutting off the hand that gives is a terrifying notion, and those who wished for it, who didn't participate in the system, deserved their punishment. As did Didem Yaylalı …

Our long run is about to end. But what's this! Five women cycling on the pavement. Lined up in a row, they come straight at me. Spreading my hands, I gesture as if to ask, "Are you serious?" They race by. I grow angry. I assume that I've finished my run, albeit with a touch of indignation, but I know upon arriving home that I was wrong. There's a tweet on my feed concerning the incident:

"Miss Temelkuran was quite disgruntled on seeing women in headscarves riding bicycles in a district like Bebek!"

How they recognised me is another story – one worth telling in its own right, considering current events in Turkey – but to be accused of being disgruntled by headscarf-wearing women in a high-end district like Bebek … now that's a remarkable story! Let me tell it …

THE BLOODIEST FRONT
IN SOCIAL PROJECTS

"So who will be debating with me on this programme?"

"We don't have her yet. We're looking for a headscarf-wearing writer or journalist."

I've lost count of the times I've received the same answer to this question about the TV programmes on which I've been invited to appear since the early 2000s. During AKP's second term, after 2007, the question was often asked behind the scenes at newspapers:

"We need a headscarf-wearing columnist. What are our options?"

The papers and TV channels knew that they needed to set up role models for their display windows that were in sync with the administration's social project. Those who fitted the profile were meticulously selected. Whereas women who had the right look and dress but not the necessary obedient reputation were mutely pushed to one side, headscarf-wearing figures hand-picked by the ruling party and its supporters began showing up in newspapers, on TV and later in Parliament. What led up to this was not only pitiful but also nauseating as far as human dignity was concerned. Headscarf-clad women were put on the front lines to "circumvent" the previous modernist social project. Catfights arose between headscarf-wearing and uncovered women on TV and in the papers. Everyone loved to see two women get into a fight. Whatever the content of the debate, this was the picture:

"Headscarf-wearing woman versus uncovered woman! Who will destroy whom? Modern Turkey or conservative 'New Turkey'?"

First, I have to admit that I've taken part in a couple of these "spectacles". I was a much sought-after figure for such "brawls" due to being selected as the "most-read female columnist" several years in a row. Also, I think, since I stood for every-thing unconventional, I also represented all that needed to be "vanquished": young, feminist, democratic socialist, rejecting the demure behavioural codes ascribed to women in public space, not soft-spoken (as sensible ladies ought to be), writing about the Kurdish and Armenian issues, not devoted to any political camp, critical of the administration to overseas audi-ences, etc. etc. ... I almost forget the most important part: I was not among the writers who lined up and sang in time to the song of "democracy finally arrives in Turkey" when AKP first rose to power. Consequently, the cycling girls on Bosphorus had plenty of reasons to commit my face to memory. I was one of the first in the popular press to be beheaded when the time came. The justification for it wasn't that I was uncovered or any of the reasons listed here. I said the wrong thing at the wrong time. Here's the story about my horrible timing.

Thirty-four people, nineteen of whom were children, were taken for "terrorists" and killed by bombing raids in Roboski on the Iraq border of Turkey. After the incident, which would become known as the Roboski Massacre, the Prime Minister's office not only refrained from making any statement, but also barred all media outlets from reporting on the matter. So, on the last day of 2011, I wrote the following article.

* * *

We get it. You wish to kill children freely while we stand by silently, saying, "They must have their reasons." You wish to bomb people and have us quietly load them onto mules, take them away to be buried … you use bombs worth a billion dollars to kill us but let us carry the coffins of our dead on our shoulders, on foot, over the snowy hills. You wish that you can just shoo us to our homes before we can accept condolences or make our elegies heard, to gnaw on sunflower seeds as we watch actors act on TV, to turn into idiots or, better yet, turn into nothing, and go off somewhere to die, and make no noise doing so, and leave no trace behind to trouble you.

We get it. You want that when an earthquake brings our homes down around our ears and you put us in nylon tents in the freezing cold and you come to us and grin, "You're living in a palace, you are!," we bow our heads and not feel the cold at all, we sell without shedding a tear the "unworn" shoes of our babies when they freeze to death, and use the money to buy sunflower seeds to gnaw on when we return home to stare at the actors on TV, to be idiots, to freeze to death quietly one night so we give you no more trouble, so we don't even have a headstone that can be an irritating reminder for you.

We get it. You want that no one knows anyone else's business, that no one concerns themselves with anyone else, that informers, children discontent with the state of the nation, angry teachers, union members, lawmakers and whoever else may stand in the way of your "thinking big" live out the rest of their days in prison, their pens and papers replaced with provisions, unable even to communicate with one another, like animals. You want that we disregard it all, go on living as unperturbed as pigs with our sunflower seeds and TV sets, while you unremittingly go on cutting ribbons at the openings of your "projects", that it's all ribbons and balloons and seeds.

We get it. You wish that you can say something one day and another the next, that one of you tells it one way when another tells it another way, that you can talk of peace and then war and then peace again, then war again, with intermittent talk of initiatives, closures, or whatever springs to mind, as we "refresh" our memories every single day, wake up to a blank sheet every day, like a mirror, never reasoning, your word our primer for the day no matter what it is, your last word our last. You wish that we doggedly trust you, that we ignore everyone else, that you're always right, then are once again proved right, so that we can sit there like dolts and say, "But wait, there's the balcony speech, have to watch that as well," reaching for our sunflower seeds, our eyes scanning the balconies for you, blind to all else.

We get it. You want that you can pitch illusionists against one another for the sake of smoke and mirrors, juggle intelligence and conspiracies to make people forget that they buried their children just the previous day, never apologising, God forbid you apologise, let our children be the butt of your children's jokes, serve your "big thinking" dead or alive, let prissy quarrels over prestige with other countries surpass the importance of our fury, let a couple of broken display windows in Istanbul annihilate the lives of our children. You can have our children who had to smuggle cigarettes across the border for money to attend prep school and died before ever having a chance to see the display windows of Istanbul, they're all yours to take, and when you cannot, you want that you can descend upon us and that we await for you to descend upon us, breast and bosom bared.

We get it. That's what you wish. You made sure we committed it to memory, and we do thank you for that! Now look in the mirror, commander. That's you! This is who you are. This is what you amount to. Now hear this, oh exalted commander! We comprise the remainder of this nation. We get you. Now what you need to get is this: that's all you get from us! We refuse! We defy! You can command all you want! Talk to yourself all you want! We are not listening!

* * *

Let me put it this way: The article was published on the last days of 2011 and I was unemployed as we entered 2012. The chief editor's call to me lasted thirty seconds. "You know why," he said, and I replied, "I do." It was a bad time to get fired. The ones who would usually have raised their voices were silent. The Kurdish movement was lying low due to the peace negotiations with the government. The left was scattered. And, after all, the patriarchal press never has been one to speak out when women are sacrificed.

Just a few weeks before, I had written an article in defence of Banu Güven, a colleague who had been fired for similar, political reasons. An article defending me was likewise written by columnist Nuray Mert. She too lost her job two weeks later. We made the cover story of a magazine with some of the swankiest and most triumphant of our old photos. It seems funny in hindsight. Those who did not know the story would never take these three insouciant women for victims.

The following period was worse than just being unemployed. AKP trolls started perpetuating lies about me over social media. Snob, spoiled, ignorant, lying, militaristic rich girl. I can't say I would have minded in those days if the last adjective, at least, had been true.

That's how the great agony started, and it went on for two years. No one at the time knew that AKP was employing – and paying – trolls on the internet and no one believed me when I told them. The precedent of what would beleaguer multitudes, the experiment of "social lynching", was being digitally practised on me. I remember a thousand people ridiculing me on social media networks when I claimed that this was a psychological weapon of war. I once read that Eskimos sat in a circle around an offender and pointed and laughed as a form of punishment. I came to thoroughly know how that Eskimo felt. Since "intellectual alignment" had not yet given way to the trend of dissent, at the time I was quite alone. And the worst part of it is that, as I retell this today, just as I did then, I'm overwhelmed with guilt. Just like the guilt and shame of brutalised women ... They did this not only to me but also to a wide array of people. Thankfully, after the Gezi protests, such lynchings have become not a source of shame but almost one of pride. It is no longer as easy to disgrace public figures through such lynching campaigns as it was in the past. As we all know, however, even when apologies are made for past crimes, those who stayed silent about the crime never apologise for their silence.

Let me wrap it up by saying that this is how the cyclists in Bebek know my face. Yet the issue, in truth, has nothing to do with my face or me. The issue is that women are being used as cannon fodder on the front line of social life, which is the most critical area during the reassignment of capital in accordance with the interests of the pro-AKP masses. Didem Yaylalı, the prospective judge who committed suicide, was an obvious victim of this story. In a way, she was a victim of the conservatives' "exaggerated fabrication" of victimhood and resentment. So adept were the conservatives in revising popular history in the wake of AKP's rise to power that everyone who unblinkingly supports AKP today is sure to tell a strange story. According to them, Turkey up until now has been ruled by left-wing powers. The "religious" have suffered the worst strife of all. The biggest victims of 12 September 1980 military coup are not the thousands of left-wing youths who were tortured but "the Muslims". A discourse of abracadabra waits ready for those who do not approve of a historical record where they are not the only victims.

Sure, people have been beaten to death for not fasting, but what do you have to say about the young women not allowed to attend classes at the university because they wear headscarves? And such.

Working like a historical resentment production centre, AKP uses its incomprehensibly strong organisation to make sure that its lowest-ranking soldier has committed this discourse to memory, until its resentful, furious followers are as ready as infantrymen. A social media analogy perfectly describes the situation:

"Arguing with an AKP supporter is like playing chess with a pigeon. No matter how well you play, the pigeon ultimately knocks down all the pieces!"

Women, unfortunately, are the most visible players in this social clash since they bear – or don't bear – their insignia on their heads. It's as if they have always felt belittled and scorned. That's why, even when they traverse Istanbul's poshest neighbourhoods in the most luxurious cars and the most expensive clothes, they are still the most victimised. And if uncovered women should direct a negative word or attitude towards them, that's the greatest political error. A woman of the richest order of the new conservative bourgeoisie class is still more of a "victim" than a retired teacher in secular attire (whatever that means) living in borderline poverty. That is why, if you happen to see them in the form of five cyclists coming at you and you, as a member of the "Republican elite", are wearing leggings for running, you need to know your place and keep quiet. Could it be that you cannot tolerate headscarf-wearers in the city's richer districts?! You would do well not to honk at a headscarf-wearing woman in a jeep when she disregards the traffic rules. Or is it that you would rather a headscarf-wearing woman did not drive … and so on and so on. The most painful part is that the numbers of those who are aware that they are sisters pitched against one another in an altogether unrelated power struggle are very small on both sides. They still are. Headscarf-wearer or not, those who proclaim that the issue lies with capital changing hands and decide accordingly are absent both on TV and in the papers. For such an approach would harm the rhetoric of exaggerated victimhood. The worst consequence of this situation is the power-hungry exploitation of stories of young women who were barred from entering university because they covered their head. Hidayet Şefkatli Tuksal, a writer and academician who always has a clear view of the matter at hand, approaches the issue thus:

"Currently, they are working at creating a wealthy Muslim class that supports Erdoğan. The administration has fattened up the contracting sector. This issue of 'wealthy classes created by the administration' is a policy that hails from the very first days of the Republic and we have already suffered its consequences as a nation."

She, I think it's worth adding, is a headscarf-wearing woman. I should also mention that she too was fired from her job at a pro-administration newspaper on the grounds of her criticisms. I doubt that any of the young women who rode their bikes at me in Bebek would know who Hidayet Şefkatli Tuksal is.

But I wouldn't want to give the incorrect impression that everything was fine and well in Turkey and we had social peace until AKP came and wrecked it. It was almost completely the opposite: everything in Turkey – social life, politics, jurisdiction, legislation, the state institution, civil rights – had all degenerated so much that the advent and acceptance of a machine of vindictiveness and spite such as AKP were made perfectly possible. The 1980s promise that "a generation without ideology" would be raised had been kept, ultimately enabling the rearing of a generation that "held onto their grudges", just as the Prime Minister wished. The outcome of the 1980 coup in terms of economic politics, political ethics and compliant conservatism, AKP's rise to power was a natural occurrence in the course of history and carried that occurrence to its next step: the absolute intolerance felt by one social group towards another. To understand what this is, let us drop in on the news during breakfast. Sure, you can turn on the TV or open a newspaper, not that that would be of any use. To know what is really going on in Turkey you need to look at Twitter. It is guaranteed to be a glum affair! But first, you must learn how to handle the experience. It won't be your run-of-the-mill process of news procurement. We are entering a tunnel of horror full of storms, adventure, gore, greed and lies. Are you ready?

A SPLIT-MEANING, SPLIT-SCREEN WAY OF WATCHING: NEWS HOUR IN TURKEY

You have showered and breakfast is ready; the morning news broadcast is about to begin on TV. It is not enough to turn on the TV, however; you must also put beside it your smartphone or computer. That's the only way you can crack the cyphers being broadcast via the TV screen. Aha! My father calls.

"Ece?"

"Dad?"

"What does this *hashtag* mean?"

"The sign for sharp notes that's on your phone screen, Dad. That's what a hashtag is. You type in a hashtag and a certain subject to see all the tweets on that subject … Tell me, what are *you* looking for?"

"Oh, I see, I see. OK."

That's how he always rings off. Bam! It's not because he's seventy-four years old, but because it angers him that he needs to gain better technological prowess in order to access news about his country. For he, like me, only sees a man hollering whenever he turns on the TV:

"Listen here, European Union!"

Having always hollered when he was Prime Minister, Recep Tayyip Erdoğan, now President, continues to holler:

"Listen here, Pope!"

He's like this whenever there is someone for him to challenge from afar:

"LISTEN HERE!"

Then he begins admonishing at the top of his lungs. Sometimes he recites a poem at the top of his lungs. Yes, he does do that.

*   *   *

Here come the awaited responses on Twitter. No one names names; they don't even reveal the sex of the subject thanks to the gender-neutral pronouns of Turkish:

"There he is again!"

"There he goes again, yelling!"

"Give us some peace, man!"

"What's he yelling about now?"

Hundreds and then, abruptly, thousands of questions are tweeted and answered, a commentary provided on the words coming from the screen and the newest victims that they target as communication clusters form. A minute is the most it takes before the sermon that still continues on screen is being teased mercilessly.

In the second news item, a minister unvaryingly promises "the severest punishment for the perpetrators" of an awful case of child molestation, the horrifying murder of a woman or the mass killing of labourers in an industrial accident. The Prime Minister, ministers, authorities … they all retreat out of sight and off screen at the end of their allocated minute without answering any questions or even being directed any of real import.

In the meantime, those at their Twitter accounts check their feeds about the hearings in the same way as people living in a normal country check their diaries at the beginning of a normal day. Every day there is invariably a class action with multiple defendants. Students who have been detained for months for protesting, or lawyers who have been unlawfully arrested for resisting the police, families of labourers who died by the dozens, activists, military men, journalists … there is invariably a trial. That's what hashtags are for – so you can keep tabs on "the trial of the day".

On yet another subject – say, news of village women protesting against hydroelectric power plants or forested areas being unlawfully sold off to people with ties to the government – yet another minister repeats the same statement for the thousandth time:

"No one is more sensitive to the issue than we are!"

In the background, nameless women and men whose voices are heard only in the form of screams as the police drag them around by their hair. As it is, the news programmes deem it worthy to show crazed people only after they've been made that way, leaving out the part about why they're crazed. For a more accurate interpretation of what's going on, you need to hunt for a hashtag on Twitter and read what's written there. But, of course, there's something you need to watch out for: trolls! They are smarter, more agile and much better at changing disguises than you think. You could even come across one who tries to pose as one of the victims to prompt you to say something about her. It's kind of confusing. But this is war and it has been going on for some time. I'll get to that.

We are at the end of the news bulletin. After the customary item about a traffic accident, it ends. Since they cannot broadcast as much political news as they would like – for TV channels that are thought to cover too many stories concerning opposition parties are immediately subjected to an onslaught of taxmen – this traffic news is the most indispensable part of the bulletin. Alternatively, some bulletins use YouTube videos of funny animals as filling. So are journalists such cowards? Are Turkish journalists too docile? Is that why it all falls on Twitter? It's not like that. Let us unearth some Twitter history as well as recent press history. However, by reading up on these two brief histories, we shall also be reading up on the history of a third and much more significant issue. "Follow me, please."

As I said, things were not so marvellous before, either. Leaving aside the events leading up to the coup, the press in Turkey was reorganised in terms of capital–press relations starting in 1980. With the permeation of big venture capital into the press, two main media groups were formed. As the values of a consumerist society and free market morality grew more widespread, there was a shift in both the gaze of the press and its standing. It now mirrored what was catchy, cheerful and rich, the media organs changing their locations from their origins outside the city to the central plazas. From where it stood, the press had a limited view. Journalists now only glimpsed the poor from afar, in their homes at the sides of the highway, as they clambered onto shuttles to go to their offices. Poverty, injustice and the struggle for civil rights were all obsolete, "old leftist" issues. The policy of censorship that started in 1980 reached a tipping point with the Kurdish issue in the 1990s. A journalist had to speak for the state, guard its sensibilities, and tread carefully lest she be labelled a traitor. And those who did not … if you were unable to find work with either of the two leading media groups, you would go hungry, which meant that the rules were set by the magnates. For the capital that owned the newspapers and TV channels also had roles in other sectors. Mining, oil companies, natural gas companies … all the magnates owned stocks in sectors dependent on the administration's approval. Therefore, those who reported "wrongfully" could be removed from their positions to make sure things ran smoothly in the mining, oil or natural gas industry. By putting off unionisation and proper organisation, press workers displayed their share of irresponsibility. Those who worked at independent newspapers and did not give in to the political authority were simply killed. Of the journalists who were killed by assassination or torture in the 1990s, Çetin Emeç, Uğur Mumcu, Ahmet Taner Kışlalı and Metin Göktepe were the most noted. The dozens of bombings, kidnappings and unsolved murders targeting the Kurdish press never aroused enough interest; for the most part, they didn't even make the news in the "Turkish" press. By the 2000s, "dissident journalism" was already a dangerous and old-fashioned trend. The political authority had no trouble establishing its own media. Government-affiliated businessmen were provided with preposterous subsidies in order to buy Turkey's oldest press institutions, whereas newspapers disassociated from the government were made to hire government-affiliated writers and journalists through "special calls" from the authorities. Facing the threat of having their capital in other sectors confiscated, newspaper and TV station owners could do nothing but step back. This resulted in the current state of affairs: today, when you turn on your TV, out of dozens of stations you see only a couple that present the news they wish to, and then with timidity and constraint. The rest are full of religious debates or political discussion programmes arranged by the spin doctors of the administration, consisting of everyone agreeing with one another. Watching these programmes is especially amusing; as everyone is in agreement, there is no actual debate or argument. The inscription displayed in the rear windows of taxis for years turns out to be right:

"Serenity is in Islam!"

The newspapers are another story altogether. Some days the Twitter community gets its morning kicks from making fun of the fact that the headlines of all the papers are identical. The headlines generally tend to be a statement made by "the Chief".

In the midst of all this, in October 2011, there was a great earthquake in Van, a city in eastern Turkey mostly populated by Kurds. TV crews reporting live from the area began making a news story out of the inadequacy of relief efforts, since they had not yet been instructed in "what not to say". Thus began the real earthquake. Recep Tayyip Erdoğan asked for reporting on the issue to cease. Incidentally, this is how this usually works. The chief editor of the paper or TV executive receives a phone call, and a voice says:

"Chief is dissatisfied."

That's all. The editor or executive knows who "chief" is and what to do. The papers and TV channels fall silent. Then what happens, you ask? That is when Turkey first discovers Twitter as a communication device. People trapped under the rubble in Van tweet, "My batteries are dying," and give their locations. Or tweets start coming in complaining of the inadequate organisation of relief efforts. Suddenly all of Turkey is organising aid campaigns over Twitter or tweeting about the administration's incompetence in the situation. News of the babies who freeze to death in the nylon tents given to the earthquake victims surface only on Twitter. The administration's "beef" with Twitter and its use as a vehicle of mass organisation start on the same day.

First used by Turkey's masses during the earthquake in Van, Twitter's political use on a mass scale happened a year later, in September 2012. It was one of the trials of a group of students; at first glance, it resembled one of the anti-terror trials that seemed to be filed daily. Its content, however, was extremely significant in light of Turkey's recent history. Because …

I don't suppose that the collective and gradual retrogression of peoples into unscrupulousness and depravity, or – let me put it this way – the legitimisation of unscrupulousness and depravity, will ever be a subject for scientific research. The notion that silent heartlessness is complicit in crime will perhaps stay between the covers of Márquez's *Chronicle of a Death Foretold*, to be considered merely a literary device. Yet this is how history should be written. This is the only way people will come to recognise the footsteps of fascism as they approach. If such a study of history existed, the date when Turkey lost its heart once and for all would probably be 31 May 2011.

The location is Hopa, a small town in the Black Sea region. The Prime Minister encounters a small band of protestors on his way into the town. They do not want one of the hundreds of hydroelectric stations to be built there, but despite court orders the private sector's influence has ensured that it will be built. The Prime Minister loathes protests. Knowing this, the police shower protesters liberally with tear gas. The retired teacher Metin Lokumcu suffers a heart attack triggered by the gas and dies on the spot. The following days, when a journalist had enough courage to ask the Prime Minister about it, he responds:

"Then, of course, one of them – I don't know his identity, I don't care to dwell upon it – died of a heart attack."

It shook social media. Students could not accept the "heartlessness" with which the death of a retired teacher was received. In return, "AK trolls" attacked everyone who voiced an opinion on the matter with the most unspeakable accusations. What most of them said was this:

"He was standing up to the Prime Minister, so of course he had to die!"

I think that that was the first day when Turkey clearly and collectively witnessed the bloodcurdling state that mass hysteria had reached. The dialogue that transpired a few days after the event between journalist Ruşen Çakır and the Prime Minister on live TV was a milestone in the history of unscrupulousness:

RÇ: I … have something to get off my chest … without talking about it, asking about it … actually … I am from Hopa, as you must know. The deceased … may he rest in peace … Metin Lokumcu is my relative. We were devastated. In every sense, all my relatives and my acquaintances too. Of course, due to your … the events there, I found out through your friends what happened. In the end, a completely decent person died in a very unfortunate manner. He was someone who taught for years in your hometown. He died in an unfortunate way and your first … response … it really astonished us. It astonished me and my family, and my relatives. I'm sure you have thought it over in the time that has passed since. Is there anything you'd like to say?

PM: First of all, of course, I'd like to give you my condolences on account of his being your relative. But let my friends, God willing, procure some pictures and some sound recordings for you. When you listen to those sound recordings and see those pictures, I think you'd concede that, even if he is your relative, is this any kind of behaviour becoming of a retired teacher?

RÇ: [In a hopeless tone that leaves several seconds of silence in the studio] But he died, sir.

PM: I don't know about that. All I'm saying is this. Because at this point I find it unbecoming for a retired teacher to be making such statements and I don't want to see a retired teacher with a rock in his hand. Because I'm the one in front of those rocks, those rocks are being thrown at me and I am the Prime Minister of the Republic of Turkey.

No TV station aired the news of the first hearing of the students who were incarcerated for four months for protesting against this reaction and against Metin Lokumcu's death. For that reason, 9 December 2011, the day of the hearing, was the first time the masses used Twitter to follow a political trial. Not everyone was growing unscrupulous, but most of us were flabbergasted at the rate at which ordinary people were. The flabbergasted began talking via Twitter. The hearing, which went on until late that evening, together with the thousands of tweets sent were the first signals of the uprising that would begin one morning two years later. My father, too, would call me two years later, after having gone on Twitter for the first time early in the morning of June 2013, and say:

"I'm on Twitter. Do you see me?"

When the Gezi uprising started millions like my father were now ready to give voice to the years of anger, pain and sorrow they had accumulated in front of their screens. The invisible had started becoming visible, even if only through nicknames and multi-coloured egg icons on their profiles. Turkey was not only comprised of those who said "He was standing up to the Prime Minister, of course he had to die!" after all, was it? Did we see one another? Twitter's most important function in Turkey was this. People longed to show themselves and one another that the country did not consist merely of unscrupulousness. Seriously, not everyone could have become part of this cruel insanity, could they? There were still among us those who retained their sanity and thought that all this was deranged, weren't there? In truth, everyone was asking of everyone else:

"Do you see me?"

* * *

I'd say that's enough breakfast and news. What do you say we go to the city centre for some coffee with friends. Like we're normal people living in a normal country. Are you ready for what we will encounter when we get in the cab?

Oh, if you want to zap through the channels before you turn off the TV, please stop a while on this one. Yes, yes, that one! The one where everyone's dancing and singing, where the housewives who constitute the studio audience thrust themselves in front of the camera and belly dance maniacally. That channel, it's called Flash TV – and it's an entirely different planet! A channel that deserves to be the main subject of Milan Kundera's book *The Festival of Insignificance*. Everyone on this channel is belly dancing from dusk till dawn. No matter what happens in the country. It's unbelievable. Perhaps we should have known the nation had truly gone crazy a few years ago once people started belly dancing on this channel twenty-four hours a day. Anyway, let's go out and hail a cab.

GODDAMN IT!

"Are you working?"

An expressionless face. The young cabbie doesn't cast a glance in my direction but appears to nod "yes".

"Good morning!"

Another nod that could be construed as, "Yeah, cut the crap."

"We're going to Cihangir."

Sighs in exasperation.

The young man, in his early twenties, is like a showpiece of passive aggression with a special emphasis on scowling and sulkiness. Not to mention that even while saying next to nothing, he manages to make me feel as though I'm responsible for his great unhappiness. In an angry motion he turns the volume on the radio all the way up. The song fits the situation:

"God damn you!"

Anger in love songs is nothing new. Written in a male-dominated language, Turkish love lyrics tend to echo the sentiment conveyed by the melodramatic phrase inscribed on the backs of trucks: "Either you belong to me or to the black earth!" The patriarchal mindset of Turkey bestows upon men permission to kill by declaring them the biggest victims, boosting their victimhood through the fact that they are now murderers. It must come as no surprise that a nation with such love songs and bumper sticker slogans has authorities that love their citizens to death.

The increasingly coarse expression of victimised or entitled fury has appeared in more recent times. Just like the one in the song that's currently playing:

No one can take away the hatred I have (for you)
Let death come if it may
I still love you
God damn you!
God curse you to Hell!

No matter what, one only falls in love in one's native language. Following the 1980s, our native tongue turned into a battlefield. It was a battle that was equal parts political, historical and societal. That even our relationships are literal battlefields has much to do with this. Not many people might readily attribute the stuttering self-destructive tone of popular love songs to politics, but the link is there. Turkish is a language that has been maimed to make sure the Kurdish could not speak

Kurdish, the left could not speak of ideology, women could not fight for their rights, workers could not resist, and much more. It behoves me to relate how the Turkish language was pauperised and made schizophrenic by the hand of government. Let me give you a single example to demonstrate the depth of impossibility in which the politics, philosophy, romantic relationships and friendships of a people who can't speak their own language flounder.

After the military coup of 1980, hundreds of Turkish words were prohibited. Banned from state TV, these words were gradually dropped from use in social life as well. They include:

active, activity, answer, artificial, artwork, aural, clause, compound, compromise, concerning, conservative, contract, coordination, critical, describe, determine, dynamic, experience, experimental, export, for instance, foresight, free, freedom, honorary, imaginary, imagine, import, international, interview, legal, life, masterpiece, memory, modern, modern woman, movement, nation, national, nationalist, natural, natural food, nature, necessity, obligation, obligatory, opportunity, partisan, peace, probability, proof, recall, recollection, relation, religious, revolution, scribe, sculpture, simile, sociological, speech, spiritual, story, structural, theory, vacation, verse, visual, vital, whole

Some of these words were replaced with their Ottoman, Arabic or Persian counterparts that had been used prior to the

Republic. These words, however, either had no equivalent in the imaginations of Turkish-speaking people or were hazy at best. That was the start of the Turkish speakers' pitfalls in communicating with one another. Then there were some words that were banned completely, one of which had a profound effect on Turkey's history:

Resistance!

After the word "resistance" was banned on the state channel, those more royalist than the king dropped it altogether. Those who forget words surely also forget their meanings and the actions they imply. It must be so. Now even Turkey's love songs are stricken with such impoverishment.

"Could we turn down the radio a bit, please?"

Snap! He turned it off completely. If you are a woman and a cab driver in Turkey has already treated you like this, there is only one thing you shouldn't do, but I always inadvertently make the mistake:

"You didn't have to turn it off. I just asked …"

As my voice fades out due to the withering glare directed at me in the rear-view mirror, he barks:

"Doesn't matter!"

He huffs and puffs. He is like a secret agent hired that morning to drain you of your will to live. It's one of the secret weapons of Turkish men: to make you feel awful for no reason. The second thing you mustn't do at this point is this, but it's difficult to refrain from doing it:

"Excuse me, is something the matter? What is there to carp about? The destination? Or that I asked you to turn down the radio? What's your problem?!"

This outburst only causes the vehicle to suddenly accelerate unreasonably and proceed in sharp, dangerous swerves. You let loose your grand finale as you're flung this way and that in the back seat:

"Could we slow down a bit, please!"

With a screech of the brakes, the car stops.

"Get out!"

"Excuse me?"

"Get out, lady!"

This incident with the taxi is not universal but is somewhat typical. Over time, you've learned not to get into arguments with highly strung drivers. Considering Turkey's recent history, you know it's the smartest thing to do. Let's meditate on this. How old is our driver? Say he's twenty-five. That means he was born in the early 1990s. Militarised by a coup when he went to primary school, educated in a conservative fashion. What that schooling process demanded of him was that he should not express himself. All his teachers were aligned with the coup, role models who never told him that he had free will, that he should care about and act in solidarity with others. He probably didn't read a single book after middle school that wasn't for homework. And assuming that his approach to women was defined by a conservative popular culture … all he did in his adolescence was hang out in coffee shops, which stopped him from communicating with any women. He was sent off to serve in the military at eighteen. If especially big and healthy, he was most likely sent to the south-east, where the Kurdish–Turkish conflict is most intense. Back home he was greeted by unemployment and landed himself a last resort job as a taxi driver. Bearing in mind that, with few exceptions, every Turkish man is put through the ruse of obligatory military service and that, for the past forty years, said service involves fighting a constant yet unnamed war, how much of the population of Turkey do you think might be suffering from Vietnam syndrome? Also, taking into account the acquaintances affected by these young men's Vietnam syndrome, what percentage of our population do you think might comprise psychiatric cases created by an unnamed war? It's a statistic about Turkey that will never be known. What we do know is that, although the taxi driver may not know it, he might be suffering from Vietnam syndrome, displaying this passive aggression because all the words he needs to describe it have been banned. Furthermore, since for him women are the most threatening thing in the world, we are bound to have to face such situations. Besides, even if he *did* have the words and *did* decide to talk, there's another prohibition in the way: the Law Against Alienating People from Military Service! In Turkey, you are forbidden from speaking out against the military or obligatory military service, and if they – especially the press – say that you have done this, you will be in some serious trouble. Let's take a look at the Turkish Penal Code:

> ARTICLE 318: Anyone who instigates, recommends or spreads propaganda that results in discouraging people from performing military service shall be sentenced to imprisonment of from six months to two years.
>
> If the act is committed through press and publications, the penalty shall be increased by one half.

Would you want to go on a car ride with a young man at the wheel who was first made ignorant, then savage, then repressed and silenced? Me neither. Let's get out of this cab. Surely we'll find another one to take us to meet friends in Cihangir. Let's talk about *that* while we wait for the new cab. It's a bit of a riot.

Cihangir is the Soho of Istanbul. And yet it's the tiniest neighbourhood. Although just ten years ago it was home to transvestites and bohemians, it gradually turned more bourgeois-bohemian. It started brimming with cafés and became a rich neighbourhood in the middle of Istanbul. A neighbourhood preferred by those working in the arts or the media. Ten minutes by foot to Taksim, the heart of Istanbul. It doesn't look like much and most flats aren't in great condition, but the highest rents in Istanbul are found in this neighbourhood. The reason is simple. There's overwhelming demand. For this is one of the few neighbourhoods in Istanbul where you can drink openly, find somewhere to eat during the month of Ramadan and generally lead a more liberal life. That's why the neighbourhood keeps getting more crowded as more people squeeze in, trying to live here together. There's a serious shortage of space, with all the liberals of an entire city trying to live in the same small neighbourhood. This cramped neighbourhood is where we're going to meet our friends.

Good, a middle-aged taxi driver has pulled up.

"How can I help you, miss?"

Just the driver we have been hoping for. News broadcast on his radio, smile on his face.

"To Cihangir, please."

"Of course *efendim*."

"Efendim" is a distinctive word. If any of you have been to Egypt, perhaps you've heard that the same word has survived there too since the reign of the Ottomans. There, it can be taken to mean something like "my lord", but in Turkey it's the sign of a certain decorum, of having manners. It tells you that the person addressing you is polite, that your relationship with him will be civil. While, in European countries, social codes and requirements are roughly the same for all sections of society and more or less adhered to by everyone, in Turkey the numbers of those who practise and keep alive these social codes are steadily declining. Anger and hate have permeated even the most minute spaces of quotidian life, rendering its smallest requirements inapplicable. I feel that this has wholly to do with the loss of people's understanding of the law. The last of the many political rulerships to impose "enemy criminal law" on those unlike itself since the country was founded completely eradicated the superiority of the law and, in general, people's understanding of it. The quotidian knowledge that the strong one is always right is a mood that spreads in descending order. It's a process of moral corruption that impacts even on one-to-one relationships. It's possible, yet challenging, to see in our intimate relationships traces of the corruption triggered by the harm done to the law. It should come as no surprise that people don't adhere to traffic regulations in a country where judges can be apprehended for not ruling the way the government wishes. To be sure, staying outside this state of affairs must require a true and earnest faith in morality. This is why, today, when you encounter a taxi driver who calls you *efendim*, it makes you as sentimental and glad as though you had witnessed an honourable one-person resistance. A hero who is struggling, all by himself, against the vulgar and crude zeitgeist. Trying to put these everyday details that we unconsciously notice into words inevitably creates a sense of exaggeration. But no, I'm not exaggerating at all. Perhaps such sentiments won't be recorded in history, but they are nevertheless present in Turkey today – and, if you ask me, such minute perceptions are having a butterfly effect on our social and political history.

"Which route would you like me to take?"

My heart is awash with warmth at the driver's attitude. I act as though I would like him to know that I'm also part of the silent resistance.

"Whichever you prefer."

"Yes ma'am."

But traffic is awful.

"What is it, I wonder? Is there a demonstration around Taksim?"

"No, ma'am. They've cut off the traffic because his *Sultan* majesty is coming."

I laugh. By *Sultan* he means the President. Since his term as Prime Minister, Tayyip Erdoğan has been trying to relocate the state capital from Ankara to Istanbul, the capital of the Ottoman Empire. Since installing his "work office" in one of the palaces, the traffic is stopped to provide quick conveyance to his security army every time he comes to Istanbul. In addition to the enormous, internationally renowned presidency he built for himself in Ankara, he also uses a palace in Istanbul in a similar way. But know that if a taxi driver refers to him as "Sultan" or "Padishah", he too, among many others, harbours great resentment. Since furious resentment is an inflationary currency in Turkey, he expresses it through the sarcastic humour. Someone who doesn't speak Turkish could assume that the content of our conversation is cheery, but the taxi driver and I chat briefly about killings, lawlessness, and the fact that they will "cash in our chips soon". Then we start looking around in the traffic. There are grey daubs of paint on the walls. Each daub has scribbles of black paint on it:

"Hmmm … grey again?"

"Must it *always* be grey?"

"I like this grey, it suits my writing."

"Haven't you run out of grey paint yet?"

The taxi driver and I look at these grey daubs and laugh. Why do we laugh?

THE GREY DAUBS OF THE CITY: PROVING PRESENCE THROUGH ABSENCE

In the past two years, random grey daubs have been appearing on most walls in Istanbul. You wake up and see them one morning. Pass by the same place a few days later, and this time you see that they've been written over with mocking writing:

"Grey again, I see! Bravo! So creative!"

The thick grey paint is used to paint over the graffiti – writing and drawings – made during and since the Gezi uprising. In fact, the short history of the grey paint started when people began to paint stairs in several locations of the city in the colours of the rainbow. Somehow coming to the conclusion that the rainbow-coloured stairs were an "anarchic" predicament, the government had the stairs painted over in grey overnight. The next day, dissidents occupied the stairs once more with their cans of paint and defeated the grey with their own colours. Then it was grey again. It's actually possible to read Gezi through this rather obvious metaphor. "Gezi" and "after Gezi" are other names for this country's war between grey and the rainbow. And even after they have run out of colours to paint walls and stairs, the initiators of Gezi continue to fight the grey with their oppositional humour:

"This grey is really slick to write on!"

So what exactly are the colours the authorities would like to cover with grey? Let's ask them.

What was Gezi? In order to understand we must go back to those days, to June 2013. We must go out to Taksim.

A newlywed couple, having stayed at the Taksim Square protests day and night throughout the first week of demonstrations, hung a banner on the front of their tent with a message personally directed to the Prime Minister: "Dear sir, please let it go so we can go home and make love!" Passers-by, depending on their political stance, either giggled or raised their eyebrows. Both reactions derived from the same fact: it is not proper in Turkey to mention the act of making love in public, let alone in writing on a banner hung in the very centre of the city. However, during the occupation a joke with erotic connotations had an extremely political meaning: the Prime Minister was attacking the occupiers with conservative morality. He was implying, if not saying openly, that the "looters" staying in Taksim Square were "doing rather dirty things – God knows what!"

This was, of course, part of a larger propaganda operation against the protestors. One day there were claims that the "looters" were drinking in a mosque, another day there were accusations that protestors had beaten a woman wearing a headscarf. At some point even a secret atomic bomb production in the tents was mentioned in government supporting media. Both incidents were supposedly captured on video, but the footage never materialised. When the imam of the mosque in question testified that the protestors had been trying to find shelter for the wounded and never had alcohol, he was interrogated for speaking to the press and exiled to another, very remote, mosque.

So it was quite brave, amid all this stigmatisation, for the couple to announce on a banner that they were not able to make love due to the tear gas attacks and police violence, but that they really wanted to do it if only the police forces would retreat from Taksim Gezi Park.

This rather insignificant joke was lost among zillions of others during the days of turmoil, which started out as a protest against the development plan for Gezi Park but grew to include wider concerns about freedom of the press and freedom of expression, and about growing injustice, inequality and conservatism in Turkey. Looking back, I find the joke rather notable when thinking about the limits of disobedience. There are three broad types of rules to disobey: written laws, society's established morals, and the code of behaviour. In Turkey it is very easy to disobey any of these.

This is how easy it is to perform an act of civil disobedience in Turkey: one doesn't need to speak out against police brutality or enforced sexual morality. A pair of leggings will do.

At times, disobedience is not even deliberate – it is something that seems to happen to you, rather than something you choose. The youngest journalist ever prosecuted, Sami Menteş, was doing his job – interviewing leftist activists just after the Taksim resistance – and he ended up in prison, where he waited nearly nine months for his initial trial. Menteş was released after the first hearing and the only evidence against him was provided by a "secret witness". The "secret witness" has become quite a popular source of information in the last ten years, especially in court cases against journalists, politicians and activists. Since the secret witness's testimony is often identical to the prosecutor's claims, one might question whether these secret witnesses even exist. Turkey has the highest number of imprisoned journalists in the world – to say nothing of the thousands of political activists and politicians, among others.

Yet, this is not our topic at the moment. The topic is civil disobedience against the general code of behaviour. It is a subtler, more refined form of disobedience – yet punished equally harshly at times – and it was an important part of the Gezi uprising. It might sound like too broad a definition for an act of civil disobedience, or too grey an area, but I call this form of rebellion simply "being nice". In fact, it is quite a courageous form of disobedience if you are aware of the essence of daily life in today's Turkey.

Just like their counterparts in Tahrir, Sol and Kasbah, the people who gathered in Taksim Square couldn't articulate perfectly why they didn't want to leave the space, even when the occupation was no longer as massive or effective as it had been. They mumbled sentences like, "It was too beautiful to leave," or, "Never mind the gas or the beatings, those were the best days of my life." And most of the time, the only explanation they could offer was some variation on a theme: "People are so nice here!" They were probably not aware that, with these sweet words, they themselves were becoming part of a subtle but strong form of disobedience.

Turkey is a rough country. An ordinary Turk visiting Britain would be shocked to see the amount of time Brits waste on apologising to and thanking each other. Let alone the time wasted on waiting in a line. Except for a few individuals who are determined to maintain their own politeness against the general current, we hardly ever say sorry. And I don't mean big political "sorries" to Armenians or Kurds who have been massacred or tortured; I mean the basic, quotidian "sorry" to someone we bump into on a busy street. Apologies are a sign of weakness in a land where we pretend that bad things never happened. There may not be a straight line between spoken pleasantries and more general feelings of compassion, but neither seem to be valued in Turkey, where – according to Istanbul Bar Association statistics – a woman is killed every two days. Maybe it is the post-traumatic stress disorder of men who are obliged to serve in the military, or the rising general tension in society – whatever the reason, between 2002 and 2009, the number of women's killings rose 1,400 per cent.

In this context, it is quite remarkable that one of the most popular threads of the discourse surrounding the Gezi uprising were testimonials like this: "You know what? People at the square are amazing! Even when we are sprayed with tear gas, even when police are attacking, they say sorry if they bump into you! They do it even while we struggle for our lives! Amazing!" In Gezi, this persistent politeness was a sign of a larger philosophy: that others matter as much as yourself, and that compassion for others is not a sign of weakness.

The "otherisation" of anyone deviating from the mainstream is also a strong theme in modern Turkish life. Being too brunette; being a Kurd; being a non-Sunni Muslim; not fasting during the holy month of Ramadan; being a bachelor; being a female university student with male roommates; being a woman and laughing slightly too much– any of these may be taken as a sign of "oddness" that might be punished harshly by society. Anybody who leads a life different from the Sunni male-dominated, Turkish-militarised, profit-driven standard may face various forms of "correction", from excommunication to public beating.

Blame this trend towards cultural enforcement on the rising conservatism, or the forty-year-old war that gave the whole country PTSD, or the obligatory military service that hardened the entire male population, or harsh neoliberal economic conditions, or call it a plainly cultural thing. Whatever the reasons, Turkey is a place where acceptance of difference is becoming rare.

But in Taksim Square, and in other similar squares that joined the uprising in other cities around Turkey, diversity was celebrated and people showed that they can coexist against all odds. The secular socialists held umbrellas for anti-capitalist

Islamists as they prayed in the rain; a nationalist leftist young woman held hands with a Kurdish activist. These personal connections – however small or fleeting they might sound – seemed impossible until Gezi happened. A miniskirt-wearing young woman collaborating with an Islamist activist to secure daily supplies for the Taksim commune might sound like a romantic, eclectic dream, but that really was the case.

People amazed themselves by becoming urban guerrillas in just a few days, but perhaps they were even more surprised by the fact that they were free to be kind without fear of being counted as weak. When there is a culture of extreme violence surrounding you, and you choose to reject this mindset by just being polite, this becomes an act of resistance. In other settings, when the powers that be demand politeness, a firm stance is an act of defiance; perhaps we are more used to thinking of revolutions in these terms. But being "nice" might be revolutionary when you are encouraged – even forced – to do the opposite. In Tahrir (Cairo) and in Kasbah (Tunis) it was the same: demonstrators' deliberate and decisive kindness towards one another seemed like an attempt to heal each other's faith in humanity, which had been deeply bruised by the cruelty of the regimes.

The most awe-inspiring exemplar of revolutionary niceness that I saw was performed by the mother of a three-year-old, whom I met in a refugee camp on the Tunisia–Libya border. In the middle of the desert, with no past and no foreseeable future, the Somali mother grew a tiny garden, with heart-shaped borders made of plastic bottles half-buried in the sand. With seeds borrowed from Bedouins passing by, she was able to grow a few vegetables. When I gave a sweet to her baby daughter, despite the sand that swallowed every bit of hope and civic habits, she made the little one say "Thank you!" I stood there for a while to receive her politeness; it took a few minutes for the baby girl to say it in English. The mother was not only trying to hold onto her dignity despite the harsh conditions, but also performing a kind of resistance against the environment that had stripped her of many of the trappings of civilised living. Maybe she was even "disobeying" my expectation of her numbness. In my view, people in the Gezi uprising were doing something similar, rejecting the numbness that was forced upon them by massive violence.

Survival in Turkey requires numbness, as in any other war zone or politically polarised country where citizens are ordered to "love it or leave it". In Taksim Square, some disobedient citizens of Turkey rejected not only the notion that they should "leave it" but also the numbness; they rejected the pattern of being hostile, violent, harsh or rude to each other. Amid clouds of tear gas, they created a world they desired: a highly unlikely Neverland of niceness. Children drew pictures; a common library was established right away; stages were built for artists' performances; people brought food to share; mothers formed human chains to protect their children. Everything was shared. I remember a kid living on the streets and begging the occupiers not to leave, because, in their actions, he "saw humaneness for the first time". Abused for so long, we were savouring the taste, over and over again, of meeting and being nice.

In a country where political legal cases go on for years without a single hearing, gigantic new prisons are built to house dissidents, the "winner takes all" mentality reigns unchecked, and the uniformisation of human lives and minds is fierce, the people of the Gezi resistance were envisioning a different rule of law and a more humane morality.

Some might think it sounds like Woodstock – hippy-dippy, flower power stuff. And during the daytime maybe it was, but after sunset it was more Gaza Strip than upstate music festival. After sunset, people who looked so naive during the day were obliged to turn into warriors against police violence. And after each night, when the sun rose, it was again time to "be nice" as an act of resistance. Not giving up the politeness was an act of disobedience that was performed deliberately – at times stubbornly, I must say.

One of the most popular slogans of the time was "Everywhere it is Taksim! Everywhere is resistance!" Protestors dreamed of stretching the boundaries of the square, of extending the newly created culture out into the rest of the country.

In retrospect, I have come to think that the Taksim Square protestors were trying to restore a sense of justice in a country where that faith had been ruined completely. Disobedience is most often associated with bringing a system down or breaking a law, but the very essence of Gezi was the opposite. They were, day in day out, creating, codifying and enacting a new code of behaviour. And it was nice … very nice.

This is why the elderly taxi driver and I smile as we look at those grey daubs now. We smile in acknowledgement, knowing that those scribbles on the grey daubs are a sign of a resistance similar to our saying *efendim*.

THE MESMERISING VULGARITY

"What was Gezi?" is a query that, in light of the chaotic nature of the events of June 2013, diminishes and limits the possibility of an answer. For a more comprehensive answer, I suppose the question might be: "What did Gezi stand against?" As you may have made out from my words above, Gezi was against a political and social morality that was steadily degenerating. The fury that facilitated Gezi is partly due to the ignorance and mesmerising, stunning audacity of the masses, and the fact that it was an audacity spreading from the highest echelons of power to the lowest rungs of society. One of the best descriptions of this situation was published in a satirical magazine. When we are talking about Turkey, you must understand that satirical magazines aren't frivolous amusements but the only media through which you can follow the political agenda without losing your mind. In a country where forthright journalism is prohibited, satirical magazines as news sources have, for quite a while, proved to have the most serious political attitude. The following passage, for instance, may be quite explanatory in relation to how Gezi occurred. Let me paraphrase Umut Sarıkaya of *Uykusuz* magazine:

> But I really don't know how we as a country got from, "Not knowing isn't shameful, not learning is," to "You think you're better than me because you went and learned something, you elitist cow? You Jacobin psychopath!" When I was a kid, learning and knowing stuff were still things you were proud of. Then suddenly the whole

country is: "You see where education takes you? As if being educated has ever helped anyone!" And finally: "What do those who know x have to teach *us*." These ears of mine have even heard the sentence, "What do sociologists have to teach *us* about sociology?"! I'm seriously scared that next, those who know and learn things will be beaten on the spot. So my advice to everyone is to make like you don't know anything, just to be safe. Your knowledge in a subject that you are knowledgeable in might be insulting to someone.

Certainly, this country's intelligentsia has been made ashamed of its knowledge due to AKP's discursive hegemony during its decade of power. For, as mentioned in the passage above, the phrase "What do scientists have to teach us about science?" has started to be repeated often by the ignorant people in power. The person mentioned above who is not dependent on sociologists to learn about sociology is, naturally, Recep Tayyip Erdoğan, the Prime Minister at the time. During his term, the animosity towards the intelligentsia that had run rampant with the coup turned into animosity towards knowledge itself. Those who defended their ignorance with the most limitless vulgarity hid behind some half-baked idea of equality when they said they didn't need professional opinion. Dams burst, buildings collapsed, trains went off the rails, mines exploded, and many more disasters occurred, and yet no professionals were consulted about anything. And when they did speak, they were accused by the government of being "pretentious" and "alienated from the public". The

Gezi uprising was the "knowledgeable ones" starting to speak at long last. The educated faction of society deactivated the "crime of arrogance" in which the government had trapped them by embracing all the insults it directed their way. Humour became not only the discursive shield of the Gezi resistance but also its igniting force.

After the police attack on a couple of dozen young people on a sit-in to stop the urban project in Taksim on 31 May, first hundreds then thousands started joining the protest. For the first three days it was just Istanbul, then Izmir, Ankara and other cities joined in. After one week, the uprising spanned the entire country. People didn't have a moment to articulate properly what they were protesting about exactly. The tear gas attack was non-stop and every police action added a new reason to "resist". The most annoying part was the mainstream media's determined and mortifying silence on the subject of the outrageous violence. In less than ten days, to everyone's surprise, even the most non-political bourgeois bohemians or Bobos became experts on guerrilla warfare. Go ask anyone in Turkey how you can stop a TOMA (the police vehicle spraying water cannons and tear gas) or the best way to cure the effects of that tear gas. Anyone can offer their own list of experiences. For two weeks, the surge of adrenalin was enormous. For those "misfits" who were looking for a country to emigrate to before the protests, Turkey became the only place to be with the uprising. And as for those who were already there, they frequently told each other that they felt guilty even for sleeping for a few hours, as if they were missing out on the action. The Turkish diaspora, with a million voices, cried on social media:

"Wish we were there!" Although there were deaths, people lost their eyes and hundreds were injured, thousands of people were still enthusiastic to join the "resistance". For many, the reason was somehow the pure happiness of solidarity and the thrill of seeing oneself being strong before the cruelty of those in power.

* * *

For political humour and art, it was as if there had been a dam holding back the current for the last ten years and now the river of quality humour and resistance art was free to flow. (Go and check out the Türkiye Direniyor channel on YouTube and look for "Direniş şarkıları" to see examples.) While the biggest clashes were taking place, people were somehow able to spare a moment or two to make a joke about the police, the government and especially Prime Minister Tayyip Erdoğan. Since the ban on alcohol coincided with the resistance, each and every day of the resistance ended with "Cheers to you Tayyip!" ("*Şerefine* Tayyip!") for those protestors who drank alcohol.

So far, I guess this has been the best way to remove the disguise of the "tolerant" discourse of a perfect marriage between democracy and moderate Islam. With every joke, the authority was infuriated into showing its ugly face – something that was already there but had been invisible to many until now.

The humour of Taksim, just like that of Tahrir and Kasbah, cannot be translated, but the mechanism that made the humour and therefore the resistance possible can be articulated.

The factor that burst the dam and let the humour flow freely and made the resistance attractive to many was a simple and tiny switch in the discourse of the opposition in Turkey. Over ten years, the government had blamed the opposition for being anti-democratic, terrorists, having links with foreign countries, being enemies of religion, elitists humiliating the "real people of Turkey", and so on and so forth. After ten years of political and psychological harassment on the part of the government and its spin doctors, the opposition was exhausted on every front. All their energy was wasted on proving that they were not these things but genuine critics of the government. Which, by the way, is impossible according to the fundamentals of logic, because you cannot prove that something doesn't exist. Through the dominant political discourse, the opposition was forced to prove their genuineness before the government. So those in power were entitled to decide whether the opposition's intentions were good or bad. For ten years the opposition had to struggle with this completely disturbed mindset. But one day – on the third day of the resistance, to be exact – when the Prime Minister called the protestors "*çapulcu*" (looters), somehow everyone reached the "enough is enough" point at the same moment and said, "Oh yes! We're *çapulcu*!" The fire caught hold. All the humiliation was embraced by the protestors, exaggerated to the point where it no longer meant anything. People even put "*çapulcu*" on Wikipedia and came up with the German (*chapuliert*), French (*chapulere*) and English (chapulling) forms of the verb. From then on, they were everything that the Prime Minister called them during the protest: alcoholics, marginal, CIA spies and even terrorists. But the peak in embracing this humiliation came with the "intergalactic coup lobby"! Among many "international conspiracy theories" that the government came up with to blame the protestors, some politicians even referred to a cyberattack on Turkey. Erdoğan's consultants went as far as to say that: "There are people who try to kill the Prime Minister through telekinetic forces." It was then that the people "declared" that actually they were taking their orders from Gondor. Darth Vader was included in this secret lobby too. People were writing on the walls:

"We are the soldiers of Gandalf!"

Go and figure out the innumerable jokes that can be derived from such craziness. So the humour, and therefore the resistance, played the dominant discourse at its own game. It was just a switch from a depressing and tiring "No, we are not" to a happy and energetic "Yes, we are, sir!" From then on, their attitude was one of "Bring it on, baby!" The fear of authority was killed with the first joke, and the humour kept on kicking the fallen authority in the gut – sometimes mercilessly, I have to say. But it is very important to note that the limitless "joy" was actually an indicator of the preceding fear of authority and it was more or less proportional to it. One could tell that the limitlessness of the humour came from the limitless fear of authority that has been created by the government.

Meanwhile, the uprising was subjected to a "God knows why it happened" kind of mainstream international journalism. The youth involved were praised by CNN International for being "free from ideology", and the protests were constantly defined as "spontaneous". The uprising was described as either "secular–non-secular clashes" or cultural wars. Neither was true. They were neither "out of the blue" nor free from ideology; they weren't even free from political organisations. They happened because of the limitless fear that the authority spread for many years and the people's determination to say that they are not a crowd of children but individual adults who are free to speak. Despite the Turkish government's legitimacy due to the democratic elections, the rising authoritarianism was discounting the existence of dissidents. Gezi was a first step showing those with political power that opposition exists. It was not a clash between the secular and the non-secular, but it was certainly a clash between dismissive authority and its dissidents. That is why in Taksim the dissidents, who came from completely opposite political wings and from all walks of life, all struggled together. Those who wanted to kill each other one week before the protests were hand in hand when the tear gas was sprayed on them. The gas had some magic power: it dissolved the hatred between political factions and turned it into a united opposing energy against power.

* * *

Gezi was simultaneously a carnival of trust against the political and societal polarisation deepened by the powers that be. Factions of society that had previously turned against one another rejected the hate marketed to them by the ruling class and put on a performance of cohabitation.

With its extreme political polarisation, the chasm between social factions, an on-and-off three-decade-long civil war and many other issues, Turkey is a place where no one likes one another much. Since there are few to no common codes among the public, we all want to live with those we are like.

Turkey might be a crazy place, but it looks today as though most of the world is headed in more or less the same direction. We do our best to protect ourselves from "the other". The world tells us "Trust no one!" while simultaneously selling us security. The security of money, of information, of human relations, of health, of children, among other things. By organising everything the same way and depending on information for foresight, the world tries to remove the need for security. More and more, our Facebook profiles start to look like the information we provide our insurance companies. Or banks increasingly want to know the same things about us as prospective lovers. To take care of the security issue once and for all, we turn into a statement about ourselves.

While all this transpires, a phantom floats above the world, the phantom of security.

"Don't go down that street! The police are attacking. Go down this street!"

In the midst of circumstances resembling war, as you are running for your life, someone on your Twitter timeline with a fake handle, whom you can't remember following or for what reason, gives you some information and you trust them. You choose to trust them. You feel that there exists a unity of sentiment; you choose to believe that your interlocutor is *like you*. I feel that calling the Arab Spring a "revolution" is a stretch. I do, however, believe wholeheartedly that there was a revolution on the basis of trust, from Tahrir to Gezi. Instead of the dozens of newspapers or TV brands that invest millions of dollars to buy our trust, we have started to believe Twitter handles with funny profile pictures. Through instinct and brief experience, we have chosen to trust people instead of establishments. In Egypt, in Turkey, people with the blue glow of mobile screens on their faces were like fireflies, and there was nothing but them to light the way. No TV channel or newspaper gave us information as dependable as strangers did. What remains from those days in terms of politics is open to discussion, but the countries where such uprisings took place saw a great change in human relations, particularly in terms of trust. In Turkey today, people who participated in Gezi don't trust those who did not. People upload photographs of themselves at the Gezi resistance even on dating sites. A female friend openly admitted the other day that she "divorced her husband because he didn't participate in Gezi":

"I can't trust that man anymore."

In the countries where such movements took place, what people emphasised and wanted to be emphasised was this: we are all vastly different from one another, but we all trust each other in wanting freedom, equality and justice. We may have ethnic and religious differences, but we trust one another's conscience, sense of justice and humanity. During these movements, photographs showing coexisting dissimilarities were the most celebrated and exalted images. The photographs from Egypt and Tunisia showing youths of the Muslim Brotherhood hand in hand with liberal youths, or the umbrellas that the leftist youths at Gezi held over the Muslim dissidents as they performed their prayers in the rain ... it all said, "That's our spirit." Everyone tore out the briars of fear surrounding their homes and declared that they could live without being surrounded by walls, that they wished to live that way, trusting one another. A phantom that defended brotherhood and trust in one's fellow humans roamed over our cities in a world that taught us to fear so it could then sell us security. All that's left now may be our "cool" gas-masked photos on Facebook and a little fairy dust, but we all saw the phantom! Therefore, no one would think of someone as being crazy for "trusting people". Because, for weeks, everyone trusted that others were the same as them, or, even if they were different, that they were good people. They chose to believe and trust. They defeated not only their fear of the authorities but that of one another's differences. We cut down the briars and took a breath of fresh air. That feeling of refreshment was the reason why, despite all the pepper gas sprayed by the police, everyone felt as though they had just taken a deep, expansive breath. Nothing reeks worse than fear. To top it all, we learned that security and trust are inversely correlated. The feeling of trust grew in spite of the fact that the police attacks obliterated the feeling of security. Trust both in those beside us and in ourselves. In a way, it was like returning the feeling of security that had been sold to us and exchanging it for the feeling of trust. And everyone was gracious enough to say, "Keep the change!"

White-collar workers in multinational companies and office blocks are "subjected" to certain orientation programmes. One of these is the "free-falling" workshop held to strengthen the feeling of trust within the group. You let yourself fall backwards and are caught by the team, which is standing behind you. In this way, a ludicrous idea for teaching trust is sold to companies to then be fed to their employees. The system expects us to be naive, cheerful children and vicious, ruthless rivals simultaneously. It demands that we both trust and never trust. Does anyone really and wholeheartedly believe this deception? I don't, and I wouldn't want to think so. But we know that the system is well versed in creating a need and then selling it to us. It succeeds in selling us a false feeling of security to compensate for the insecurity it fosters in us, as though it wasn't the very thing making us rivals and thus turning us against one another. We, the world, are tired of this schizophrenic situation. We want to trust. We want to trade in the security farce for the feeling of trust.

Gezi was also an uprising against memory loss. There was a name in the earlier pages of this book that I asked you to remember. Deniz Gezmiş. One of the three youths executed in 1972. In 2013 – that is to say, forty years later – just a few days after the Gezi uprising began, the handsome face of rebellion that two coups and countless right-wing administrations sought to erase from memory covered the façade of a building on the biggest banner in Taksim Square. Next to it, on a similarly large banner, were just the words:

"Don't bow down!"

Many words resurfaced after thirty years of being pushed into oblivion, the most important of which was:

Resistance!

This word, which was ejected first from the state's vocabulary and then from the memory of the public, probably became the most used word in Turkish in the period following Gezi. So much so that even those who didn't participate in the uprising were obliged to use it. Refusing to say "resistance" was something akin to a sin. A generation born after the word had been forgotten had made it part of the Turkish language again. This time, an integral part. Likewise, the word "organisation", which, following the coup had always sounded rather illegitimate, also came back with the Gezi uprising. Solidarity, too, was back, not as an obsolete word favoured by old leftists but as a young one. They had returned in the wake of their meanings, of course.

Gezi was also a resistance against the corrupted map of meanings. It was a struggle to set everything upright after a decade that had tipped the concepts of good–bad, right–wrong and beautiful–ugly upside down. Ignorance was wrong, knowledge right; not the other way around. It was good to resist authority, bad to cooperate with it; not the other way around. These mirrored buildings were ugly, trees were beautiful; not the other way around. Turkey was redrawing its map of meanings as it ought to be.

Which brings us where, today?

* * *

After all the seismic aftershocks of Gezi had died down, a strange frame of mind remained. A silence reminiscent of a retreat to the trenches. A general feeling of numbness. A deep apathy, indifference and listlessness in relation to one's surroundings that was of pathological dimensions.

We have good reason to be like this, of course. We're like dogs beaten too often; we have received too much of an "emotional beating". This one example, among others, is sufficient on its own: struck on the head with a gas capsule at fourteen, Berkin Elvan dies in hospital a year later at fifteen and a middle-aged woman attends a rally where Berkin Elvan's family is branded as terrorists and booed by the crowd, while she declares her love for Tayyip Erdoğan, Prime Minister at the time, with the words, "I wouldn't mind being the hair on your arse!" – on live TV, no less. After this and hundreds of other "emotional beatings", the soul may want to hide, to sleep and preserve itself. But is that the reason? Or the only reason?

"We're like this because we're too beaten emotionally" comes across as a bit of a simple explanation. It's true we're reeling from the blows, but too much evasion when describing what we were after has also confused us. Not having decided in which direction to run, and therefore running in every direction, has exhausted us. Perhaps if we hazarded the question "What are we after?" – a question that was so popular at the Gezi protests – we might have a chance of changing our situation.

* * *

It's clear we're after something difficult. If we were to make a little list to describe it, it might be something like this:

- A movement that is not an organisation
- A force that is not authority
- A cooperation without hierarchy
- A presence that prefers to be unnamed
- Unpremeditated agency
- Unique individuals who yearn for affinity
- A resilient language and rhetoric that don't solidify concepts
- Fury that is obligatorily manifested as a carnival

It seems to me that we are members of a generation that is not yet defeated but unwilling to say which horse we bet on because we fear defeat so much. We are the ones who remain silent because we haven't openly declared our unique list of demands. We are silent not because of the sting of the blow to the face, or the fear of the new blow that might land, but because we are unsure of what to say.

Now, as we draw near Cihangir, the taxi driver and I both fall silent. For the cab is surrounded by Syrian children. They beg in Arabic, barefoot and multitudinous. Multitudinous … hungry … then there is this. Millions of new faces in the city's hungry, black crowds. Almost everyone feigns ignorance but another invisible city grows within Turkey; without language, without anything. We should say a few words on this before moving on to the amusing scenes we are about to witness.

CHILDREN OF THE "ZERO PROBLEM" POLICY: THE EXPEDIENT AND INEXPEDIENT

Syrian children began filing into the streets of Turkey first by the dozens, then by the hundreds, and ultimately by the thousands. Barefoot, bedraggled, hungry and voiceless. They beg in the few Turkish words they have learned and revert to Arabic when that isn't enough. The word they repeat most often is "Syria! Syria!" They know that the word now verifies their indisputable misfortune. Waiting for traffic to jam, they adhere to the windows as soon as the cars grind to a halt. Some are five years old at most. They're learning Turkish through the vocabulary of the beggar. They're too young to know that they're victims of an ambitious, delusional and completely imbalanced foreign policy. But they will soon grow up and find out that the story that has led them to scramble desperately in traffic actually originated many years ago …

It all began when the airplane flew into the tower. Recep Tayyip Erdoğan would probably become the most fortunate person to ride the wind of "either you're with us or you're the enemy" that gripped the world from 11 September 2001. He happened to be the new young Muslim leader of a democratic country, the greater majority of which, it was always said, was Muslim. He was a befitting candidate for standing behind the security concept that would influence the post-9/11 world, being the most eager cooperator in the region on neoliberal policy and cutting a figure on the world stage as the good example in the good Muslim/bad Muslim dichotomy generated by Washington. Washington was exhilarated about having discovered a more handsome role model against the "terrorist Muslims" than the Saudis. This intellectual mien was sanctioned not just in the White House but even by the most respected European universities. The Muslim NATO country Turkey had become the West's exemplary student in the East. Inasmuch as Erdoğan said "There is no moderation to it, there is only one Islam" in relation to domestic affairs, he was pleased with his portrayal as the "new leader of moderate Islam" in international mainstream media and being on the cover of *Time*. During this period, the Fethullah Gülen Community's Washington connections, in particular, were put to maximal use, since the organisation was already well versed in international relations. Reports from international think tanks practically competed with each other to praise democracy in Turkey. Oh, those sweet early days! Then the invasion of Iraq appeared on the agenda and Tayyip Erdoğan did a lot of yelling at rallies to include the Turkish army in the international occupying forces. This was prevented thanks to the efforts of the Anti-war Platform, which encompassed hundreds of thousands of people, and of which I was one of the two spokespeople, and Parliament vetoed the army entering Iraq. Between you and me, the administration has good reason for being furious with me. But although the Prime Minister was furious with the likes of me, he somehow still managed to use this decision of Parliament in his favour, even though he had no part in it. In fact, in Lebanon, where I was reporting at the time, I saw this billboard with my own eyes in a Hezbollah stronghold. Chávez and Erdoğan stood side by side as two leaders against the Iraq occupation with the words underneath asking:

"Where are the Arab men?!"

He was angry at me and people like me for preventing Turkey from playing an active role in Iraq's occupation, but the Prime Minister was being hailed on the streets of Arabia as a USA-defying hero. He also managed in subsequent speeches to act as if it were his decision not to participate in the occupation. Now that you have more of an inkling about the political manoeuvres of AKP and Prime Minister Erdoğan, you must be less surprised by such bizarre situations. This particular situation continued to exasperate those who remembered the truth for many more years, and Erdoğan found it in himself to keep giving speeches condemning the occupation of Iraq. What can I say? It was interesting!

In any case, right afterwards began the glamorous period of the AKP administration's foreign policy. "Our brothers in the Middle East," said the Prime Minister. "Cultural proximity," he said. And finally he let the cat out of the bag:

The Middle East Initiative!

The Middle East, which had been shunned culturally and kept at arm's length politically since the founding of the Republic of Turkey, now meant countries one could visit without a visa. In addition, trade was liberalised and leaders, to show off their cosy neighbourly relationships, began dropping in on each another for a coffee. A short while before the uprising began in Syria, Tayyip Erdoğan referred to Bashar Assad as "brother". A funny detail: the name, which in Turkish was *Esad* when Syria was our friend, turned into *Esed* once the Prime Minister began implementing policies against the regime. Since Esad was a name also commonly used in Turkey, a man who was now our enemy had to have a "foreign" name. Once the Prime Minister changed Esad to Esed, the entire press scurried to change the name they had spelt the same way for years. It was now forbidden to call Esad Esad! Before we look at this period of enmity, however, the circumstances during which Turkey suddenly became the Young Turk of international politics must be examined. Let's consult Professor Soli Özel, international politics expert, to understand the sudden rise of the regional star:

The rise of Turkey's international political profile happened within a specific regional and international conjuncture. The components that defined said conjuncture were the attacks of 9/11 (2001), the Iraqi War (2003), and the new balance of power in the region.

The USA's inability to control the consequences of the Iraq War caused Iraq to spiral down into violence. One of the regional consequences of the war was that Iran, with newfound influence, became a force spreading from Syria and Lebanon through Hezbollah to the East Mediterranean via Hamas in Palestine. With the USA's overthrow of Saddam Hussein's regime, the balance of power on Iraqi soil, which for centuries had been in favour of the Sunnis, was also tipped, Iran having a say in this region for the first time after around three centuries.

The new regional realities created by the Iraq War were as useful to Turkey as they were to Iran. Ankara was closely involved with developments in Iraq. Its advantage of being able to communicate with all groups enabled it to become, for a time, an influential actor. Despite all the pressure from the USA, it did not cut ties with Iran and Syria. Quite the contrary: it strengthened its economic ties with both these countries and with the other actors in the region. It endeavoured to become a mediator between Iran and the West. Aiming for a peace treaty to be signed between Syria and Israel, it made quite a bit of headway in this regard until the Gaza assault of Israel in 2009 resulted in disassociation.

I should cut in and explain. The showiest slogan of Turkish foreign policy at the time was this:

"Zero problems with the neighbours!"

Professor Ahmet Davutoğlu, who would go on to become Prime Minister, was the one who came up with this gimmick. He was the author of a book named *Strategic Depth* that experts agreed didn't have much depth. To be fair, a policy of zero problems with the neighbours sounded nice to the ears, as, since its founding, Turkey had been a lonely country that believed itself to be "surrounded by enemies". Finally the ghouls beyond the borders would vanish and we would have normal relationships with Armenia, Iran, Iraq, Syria and other countries. At least, that was the plan. It seemed to be going along quite well for a time, too. Let's turn to Soli Özel again to see what happened next:

In accordance with the principle of *zero problems with the neighbours*, Turkey took steps to clear the way for economic integration. Trade was liberalised when the requirement for visas for many countries was eliminated. As a result of both Turkish TV series that made a big impression in the region and the rising frequency of reciprocal visits, Turkey's lifestyle, democracy, prosperity and the *soft power* that had been nourished by the European Union membership process, which was believed to have helped Turkey obtain all of this, turned the country into a centre of attraction.

The fundamental approach of the policy of this period was that Turkey was the *central country* for the regions that surrounded it. With this concept, the *desire to move on its own*, which represented a deep-seated tradition in Turkey's foreign policy, came to the fore. As part of its rising profile and due to its historical, political and strategic accumulation, Turkey was supposed to produce independent and autonomous policy ...

The shift of the world's strategic centre towards the east and the power vacuum in the areas surrounding Turkey already provided Ankara with room to manoeuvre. This structural advantage, paired with Turkey's unique characteristics (as a new secular, democratic, capitalist, NATO member Muslim country), made it easier to achieve its desired aim.

The failing of these policies of the period that were to drive *soft power* forward was the aspect of security. Although it defined its foreign policy by the most intricately forged concepts and strove to transform the region and its neighbours with the help of soft power, Turkey did not have a comprehensive security policy. In comparison, as seen in the Syria example, it had few or no opportunities for dissuading antagonists.

After the Arab uprisings that began in 2011, the climate around Turkey changed once again, in an unforeseeable way. The transformation sought by the mostly urban masses who rose up with a demand for democracy did not happen. Except for Tunisia, no "Arab Spring" country remained with a functioning democratic mechanism. With the contributions of the counter-revolutionary wave originating in the Gulf, the coup of July 2013 took place in Egypt and the country returned to the old regime. Violence boiled over with the collapse of the government in Libya. Because it was not left to its own devices, Syria turned into the bloody, inhumane and disgraceful scene of a power struggle that was both regional (Iran–Saudi Arabia–Turkey) and global (USA–Russia/China).

After the Arab uprisings, Turkey naturally attracted the world's attention. It was even ascribed with role model status due to its soft power: that is to say, being a democratic Muslim country within the Western system. The right and ethical approach of this period's policies was to support the people's rebellion against despotic regimes. Ankara, however, was unable to correctly interpret the power balance in the Middle East. Despite the fact that all of them were Muslim, it was unable to determine the direction of the policies of the region's countries, which all had very different aims. Even more ironic was the realisation in hindsight, after the American troops had left the country, that the USA's presence in Iraq had actually expanded Turkey's freedom to manoeuvre.

Beyond this, Ankara, in my opinion, made two more mistakes:

1) It abandoned its supra-denominational policy that it had faithfully adhered to until the start of the rebellion in Syria in March 2011 because it was unable to persuade the Ba'ath regime to find a peaceful solution. It played a first-hand part in the Syrian civil war and let the opposition use its borders. At the end of three years, the judgement became ingrained in the world that Turkey was one of the principal supporters of Sunni jihadist components.

2) Due to its ideological proximity, AKP became too engaged with the Muslim Brotherhood administration

in Egypt. As a result, the attitude of recrimination against the coup, which was ethically and politically just, caused rhetoric to become too harsh and relations to be severed with Egypt. In addition, it drove a wedge between Turkey and the Gulf countries grouped around Saudi Arabia and added an element of unsavoriness to relations with the West.

The Gezi Park protest that took place in June 2013, a short while before the coup in Egypt, on the other hand, irreparably damaged the democratic image Turkey had painstakingly built up over the previous decade. The AKP administration's response to the Gezi Park demonstrations, the violence practised by the police and its support by the government, as well as the rhetoric used during these incidents, nullified Turkey's chances of being a democratic or even a liberal model for the Middle East.

Reflecting a serious incompetence in foreign policy, attempts were made to sublimate this state of affairs using a concept called "*precious loneliness*". Such equivocations, however, do not change the reality that foreign policy has entered a grim period of floundering and has focused on saving face.

After this lucid summary of the past ten years, it should be said that, with the floundering of foreign policy, oddly enough, it was children who paid the price. Let me explain …

The Rabaa Massacre took place on 14 August 2013. The Egyptian Armed Forces and police, under command of the coup's temporary Egyptian Prime Minister General Abdel Fattah el-Sisi, opened fire on supporters of the Muslim

Brotherhood. Seventeen-year-old Esma was among the dozens of casualties of the massacre. Prime Minister Erdoğan was so affected by this incident that he wept for Esma on live television. AKP supporters had already started demonstrating for Esma and the other victims of the Rabaa Massacre. Pro-AKP TV stations and newspapers immediately placed a hand with four fingers raised next to their logos. This was a sign suggesting the word "*arba'a*", which in Arabic means four. All this could have been interpreted as a humane and sensitive reaction, if only police violence in Turkey had not caused the deaths of six young people at exactly the same time! Prime Minister Erdoğan, who made not a peep about the youths killed by police violence during the Gezi protests, let alone shed tears for them, wouldn't stop talking about Esma. It would appear that Esma was more politically expedient than the young people at Gezi.

Many people were driven to explosive fury by this lack of remorse. Among these were Sezgin Tanrıkulu and Rıza Türmen, two parliamentary members from the opposition party CHP. According to the report prepared by these two members of Parliament, the administration's lack of remorse towards children went a long way back. This is what the report said:

"In the time that passed between twelve-year-old Uğur Kaymaz being killed in front of his home in 2004 and fourteen-year-old Berkin Elvan being killed during the Gezi protests when he left his home to buy bread, we have seen no change in AKP's child-hunting policy. All child murders, of which the most notable is the Uğur Kaymaz case, have been either unpunished or finalised with sentences that were more like prizes. Eighteen children were murdered in 2006, three in 2007, one in 2008, twelve in 2009, fourteen in 2010 and thirty-one in 2011. Of the thirty-four casualties of Roboski in 2011, twenty-two were children. Ten children were killed in 2012, one in 2013 and three in 2014. Out of the six people who lost their lives in Cizre in the events of the first month of 2015, four were children."

Despite all this, I believe the AKP administration will go down in history under the name Pozantı when it comes to children. The story I'm about to tell doesn't have a happy ending, let me warn you up front.

*　*　*

In February 2012, this news appeared on the Dicle News Agency, an independent news website, based in Turkey, which mostly covers the Kurdish issue. The news itself was actually one year old. It was about a little town named Pozantı, in Adana, southern Turkey. The events described in the report are alleged to have taken place in a juvenile prison with mostly Kurdish kids as inmates. The horrifying story was actually documented one year ago by the Human Rights Association (HRA). This organisation offered detailed descriptions of the torture that some children were subjected to during their term in prison. Seven children have produced their own written testimonies about their rape, sexual harassment and torture by prison staff and other people at the prison. Some of these kids were in the prison under the anti-terror law that treats minors as adults.

After the preliminary reports in June 2011, the Human Rights Foundation (HRF) this time prepared another report about eight children with the same allegations against the prison administration. In July 2011, HRA and HRF applied to the Turkish Ministry of Justice presenting the testimonies and health reports of twenty-five children. In these applications, the children testified that they had been raped by adult detainees, soldiers and the guards. Some of the children were not even able to describe what happened to them. One of the children's testimonies ends like this: "I was going to commit suicide but I thought of my mother and couldn't." It was not only sexual crimes that were committed against these kids. The horrific treatment included periodic beatings by the guards, ethnic humiliation, forced labour, and bastinado (a very popular and ancient torture method known as "*falaka*" in Turkish which involves whipping the bottom of someone's feet). They were also barred from receiving medical attention and were hung from a basketball hoop until they began to choke as another form of torture. The news about the children of Pozantı Prison was not even an issue for the mainstream media. It was a Kurdish issue, and the media already knew that the government didn't want to hear anything of that nature. The silence was unbearable. So the people on Twitter started a campaign to become the voice of the Pozantı kids. Under pressure, the mainstream media had to leave its fear of the government aside and started publishing news about the prison. Almost one year after the torture had been reported, the Minister of Justice made a statement about the incident.

The solution that they came up with was "brilliant". They were going to move the children to another prison and this time the prison was going to be newly painted! The ministry made a big media show about the new prison in Sincan, Ankara, in central Anatolia. The walls were painted green. There were ridiculous pictures of dolphins and flowers on the walls just to cheer up the tortured kids. Moreover, this time they were supposed to stay in separate, camera-monitored cells, each kid on his own, in solitary confinement.

* * *

So this was the delicate treatment that the Ministry of Justice thought would be suitable for raped and tortured kids. On a Tuesday in early March, 218 kids from Pozantı were transferred to Sincan, which is an eight-hour drive from Adana, where the children's families live.

Had the story ended here, it would have been just another very disturbing story about Kurdish kids. But for many years now the word "disturbing" has had a whole new meaning in Turkey. Therefore, we learned through a report released by the main opposition party CHP that the administrator of Pozantı had already been appointed to Sincan Prison by the Ministry of Justice. So he was there already, waiting for the kids when they arrived. The second administrator of Pozantı, whom the children talked about the most in their testimonies, was appointed to another Kurdish town, Van, to carry on with his accomplishments (as a promotion, nonetheless). Yet there was more to come. On the same Tuesday, a massive police operation was directed against the Dicle News Agency. The three correspondents who had written the stories about the Pozantı kids were detained on allegations of being members of the KCK, allegedly the urban branch of the PKK Kurdish armed movement.

It didn't end there. It was reported that a young man, known as TT, one of the former prisoners in Pozantı, was detained as well. He was the source who had informed the Dicle News Agency correspondents about the case. So everybody who raised his voice about Pozantı is safely locked up in prison. The kids were definitely enjoying their greenish solitary cells with dolphin pictures on the walls. Or so we thought, until a letter from Çağdaş Ersöz was published on sendika.org, a leftist news website. He was prosecuted in a trial lasting several months for protesting against hydroelectric power turbines, and in his letter he described his two months' stay in Sincan. Although there were similar rape and torture stories in Sincan, the prison was most famous for its original invention: the soft room. According to Çağdaş, everybody in the prison, including the doctors, knew about this room. Since those under the age of eighteen cannot be punished by depriving them of receiving letters from visitors, the guardians punish them in their own special ways in this so-called secret room. Beating, bastinado (*falaka*), stripping inmates naked and keeping them in the cold are just a few of the many methods of violence. Çağdaş says that on the day of his arrival, a child committed suicide in his cell and another was raped by an older detainee. So we at least know now that the Pozantı kids have their greenish cells to rest in and pictures of dolphins to dream about after the soft room sessions.

You know those scripts that appear after such movies end. For instance, they say: "The people responsible for the horror at Pozantı were found guilty and sentenced to such and such years of imprisonment." Then, as the script keeps going, you find some relief. Something will appear on the screen saying: "The kids were released and received proper psychological treatment." It is at this point that you will be able to go to bed in peace. You cannot sleep without knowing that humanity triumphs and that good overcomes evil. That is human nature. But in Turkey, you sleep anyway. You sleep just to wake up to another day to see how much further it can go and just assume that this has to stop somewhere. But it doesn't – and it didn't in the Pozantı case either.

One of the children who were raped in September 2012 attempted suicide twice. He was barely saved after lengthy treatment. Straight afterwards, he was taken into custody again and tried in court with a sentence of forty years. The victims of the 24 November 2014 incident were put on trial for "bodily injury, coercion, defamation, property damage, and resisting an officer". The four children are being tried, with life sentences hanging over them.

Say the incident troubles you and you want to go online and see what happened, or will happen, to the kids. Don't bother. The many websites that ran news stories on the subject have been banned.

The Prime Minister didn't weep for them, because they weren't children like Esma who were expedient for AKP's policy. Just like the thousands of Syrian children who roam the streets begging and have no hope of a future. The Syrian children, the children from Pozantı, aren't the kind of children you want. What kind of children do you want? Let me give an example. During the Gezi uprising, the Prime Minister held a series of retaliatory rallies. Sometimes he had three rallies in one day, he was that annoyed. One of the kids at these rallies was named Serra Zeynep, or, to paraphrase the banner she held, "Little Serra Zeynep". On the banner that was plastered all over the papers was written, supposedly from the mouth of the six- or seven-year-old:

"We want religious husbands, not alcoholics or looters."

Zeynep wouldn't take a Gezi rioter for a husband and the pro-AKP media found this so cute and important that it made headline news.

If your heart is weary and your stomach churning, let's get to Cihangir and talk about lighter things. But you might be better equipped to understand the emotions Gezi evoked in people when you see the writing on the walls of the incline leading up to Cihangir, left over from Gezi and somehow untouched by the grey paint:

"Take our damn lives! We're all dying anyway!"

Right underneath, a typical Gezi wisecrack:

"He speaks the truth, gentlemen!"

THE MEATBALLS OF "THE PEOPLE" BEAT MACBETH TO DEATH

Although Cihangir is the Soho of Istanbul and quite a wealthy neighbourhood, the roads are awful. Full of potholes. The verdict in the area is that the AKP municipality refuses to fix them in order to punish this neighbourhood as it was so prominent in the Gezi protests. It's likely, because the last time the AKP mayor attempted to visit the neighbourhood, he was heavily insulted and barred from entering. The area is famous for its countless cafés and the numerous expats who live alongside Turkey's Bobos, and one of the most renowned places is the coffee house underneath the mosque at its centre. Who frequents this coffee house, then? "These" people do. Who are "these" people? Let our Prime Minister answer; he's practically the one who came up with the phrase.

* * *

On 8 March 2012 in Kahramanmaraş, the stronghold of right-wing politics and nationalism, Recep Tayyip Erdoğan was once again provoking a crowd to exhilarated fury, although they didn't really know the meanings of some of the words he was using. The kind of speech you're about to read was a good choice for Maraş. Granted the title of *"kahraman"* – heroic – by a right-wing administration in 1973, the city is acclaimed for its 1977 massacre of Alevis. Erdoğan had picked just the spot to talk about the artists, intellectuals and journalists of Istanbul:

> My dear brothers and sisters, **these** people make art for art's sake. **These** people don't make art for the people …
> **these** people are elitist. **These** people are Jacobin. These people never allow others to enter their caste system …
> Only **these** people know about theatre. Only **these** people know about movies, music, sculpture, painting, literature.

These people look down their noses at the people, at the sweat and blood of the people, the culture and choices of the people. For years they have belittled our people with caricatures. For years they have belittled them through columns, on their screens. For years they have belittled the true servants of this nation – its clergymen …

What do we say now? What we say is, brother, you want to act in theatre? Move freely, be our guest and establish your own theatre amongst yourselves, get into this business privately … Sure, we'll provide the stages, if we should like your play our review committee can sponsor it, we can support this as well. But the mentality that brought you here shall no longer exist. Go out, move freely, be free, be autonomous, be private, but now the state washes its hands of the theatre. Be my guest and stay on your stage!

This speech is a perfect example of the discourse Erdoğan has practised for years and has had his following practically commit to memory. Given for the privatisation of state theatres – which was a prominent part of the effort to create, after conservative policy, conservative art and culture as well – this speech, one among hundreds, refers to "these people". The Turkish demonstrative adjective "these" is insulting and is used more widely to refer to things or animals, and on the lips of Tayyip Erdoğan and his followers it's always used to implicate the same social group. Yet, although this group was smaller in the beginning, it gradually grew larger as Erdoğan gained power. Connoting supporters of "military tutelage" in his first term, it steadily began to be used for those who criticised AKP for becoming authoritarian, then anyone who wasn't on their side. "These people" became an insulting expression for leftists, intelligentsia, artists and then almost everyone with an education. Whenever Erdoğan said "these people" in one of his speeches, "Boo!" cried the crowd, the hatred of the intelligentsia already latent in the country now boiling over. Every speech also helped to lay the foundations of the state's operation to persecute, ignore and ostracise the intelligentsia. "The people" was sublimated through a discourse of victimhood and essentially invited to seek revenge on "these people". After this and other similar speeches, the same thing invariably occurred throughout AKP's duration in power. Let me give a few examples.

In 2013, the Ministry of Culture began to evaluate its subsidies to private theatres under the criterion of being "suitable with regard to public decency". This enforcement arose as part of the Turkey Art Association (TÜSAK), which was put forward in a bill advocating the audition and support of art associations affiliated with the state. In this way, the legal foundation for state-imposed censorship was laid. For the evaluation of private theatre companies' grant requests to the Ministry of Culture, submission of the play's script was made obligatory.

Shakespeare's *Macbeth* was removed from the State Theatre repertoire in 2014.

In December 2014, Şevket Demirkaya, who had previously held positions such as wrestling referee and municipal police chief, was appointed Director of the Istanbul Metropolitan Municipality Theatre Company.

In 2013, the Ministry of Culture cut off its funding to the company of Genco Erkal, one of the most acclaimed stage personalities in Turkey, for supporting the Gezi protests.

The Directorate General of State Opera and Ballet prohibited the wearing of certain garments, including leggings, in October 2014.

* * *

Theatre wasn't the only thing Erdoğan had a beef with, naturally. He was also passionate about sculpture. On 8 January 2011, during election preparations in Kars – a place the whole world is familiar with thanks to Orhan Pamuk's novel *Snow* – he was once again yelling, "Freak show!"

The freak show in question was an enormous statue. The mayor, a member of his own party, was having a peace statue built in the city bordering Armenia, a statue that could be seen from Erivan. The work, by one of Turkey's most renowned sculptors, Mehmet Aksoy, had just been completed when it turned out that it didn't suit Erdoğan's tastes. A few months after Erdoğan appraised the sculpture as a "freak show", it was demolished in spite of every court ruling, and at quite a high cost. The worst part about it all was the cry of "the people" as they set about its destruction:

"Allahu akbar!"

I suppose that the intellectuals who were irked when I suggested that sometimes Turkey was like Afghanistan with a nicer shop window, who thought it "elitist and Jacobin", probably shared my apprehensions on the day they witnessed that savage and wanton destruction.

Erdoğan was also interested in music. That was why the work of Fazıl Say, a world-renowned composer and pianist who was critical of the AKP administration, was immediately removed from the repertoire of the Presidential Symphony Orchestra.

Perhaps the eeriest of these persecutions over the years came in December 2011, from the Minister of Internal Affairs. The Minister said:

"The backyard of terrorism, walking around the back, and by backyard this could be Istanbul, could be Izmir, Bursa, Vienna, Germany, London, wherever – it could be a podium at the university, an association, a non-governmental organisation ... They look like they're just singing but they say something to the audience in between three songs, squeeze in a few lovely words. Whatever you take from it, however you understand it. They're making art on that stage. What can you do? We are not against art, but we have to weed these out with the meticulousness of a surgeon."

I wish the best of luck to the translator who has to translate these words. I hope readers, too, will manage to keep their wits intact after so much of the government's poor self-expression.

In the wake of these declarations that signalled a new onslaught of custody and persecution, artists came up with a parody petition:

"Ban art! Put art within the scope of terrorist activity!"

We have said that the most crowded of the countless cafés in Cihangir is the open-air coffee house below the Firuzağa mosque. It's a traditional coffee house where patrons ironically have to look at the stone coffin rest that coffins are put on for funeral services. When the call to prayer makes it hard to hear one another, people stop talking and sip tea. The rest of the time they talk about whatever it is that artists, actors and intellectuals talk about in any other metropolis in the world. This place is also known among the Istanbul art scene as the "Labour Market". For all the theatre and TV actors are here almost all day. Ask anyone at this coffee house about the reaction of "these people" – as they are referred to by Erdoğan – to all this, and it is bound to be one of fury. But if you ask "these people" "What are the choices of the people whom you are accused of 'belittling'?", then you can have some fun.

Let's take a look at "our people's" choices.

In terms of sculpture, for instance, "our people" are faced with two dominant types. At every point and in every location in Turkey, you see sculptures of Atatürk; these have been mani-acally multiplying, especially since 1980. Atatürk on his horse, pointing out the target to his troops; Atatürk pointing young men in the right direction; Atatürk pointing young women and men in the right direction; or Atatürk standing there, not pointing. Some of these sculptures are exceptionally bizarre. In a city in Anatolia, Atatürk is shown Dracula-like, enveloping a young man in his cape. The only other type of sculpture that interrupts the inarguable hegemony of Atatürk sculptures, busts and reliefs can be referred to as "the city's famous produce". This type usually consists of a plain sculptural rendering of the province's top products. While in Malatya this is an apricot and in Diyarbakır a watermelon, it can also perfectly well be a meatball stuck with a fork in Inegol. You can see such food and animal sculptures in almost every city. The scariest of these sculptures, which are usually situated in the centre or at the entrance of a city, in my opinion, is the statue of the Van cat in Van. A gargantuan cat glares at you as you approach the edge of the city. In a movement influenced by proximity to the Arab world in recent times – due to religious reasons, this proximity also affects aesthetic references – "the people" have also grown fond of plastic palm trees. Due to what appears to be some sort of competition between AKP municipalities, these have also been crazily multiplying in various cities throughout the country.

Our people's most prominent preference in the performing arts is for game shows where the crudest, most vulgar jokes are made and where people being humiliated is the main attraction. Overall, these are so lowbrow they make the dance competition in *They Shoot Horses, Don't They?* look like the Bolshoi Ballet.

To add to all this, a small tip about Turkey: most taverns, especially ones in Anatolia, have photographs of Atatürk on the walls. Atatürk drinking, Atatürk on a swing or simply a portrait. These depictions of Atatürk hang in the best spot as icons that legitimise the drinking of *rakı* on a social scale and accentuate the secularity of the establishment.

The administration – in fact, Erdoğan in person – has also had a pop at the people's enjoyment of poetry, Erdoğan taking it upon himself to loudly recite a nationalist, conservative poem in the TV commercial prepared for the Battle of Gallipoli memorial events.

The people's taste in cinema has also been addressed, with movies with gargantuan budgets being provided by the government. The film *Code Name: K.O.Z.*, in particular, is a notable example. "Relaying" the clash between the Fethullah Gülen Community and Erdoğan supporters at the administrative level and "documenting" the Gülen supporters' treachery, the film was underappreciated by "our people", despite being shown for free, and was removed from theatres after hardly being watched at all.

The subject of literature, on the other hand, is a whole predicament on its own. In the last five years especially, rather obscure conservative writers have been sent to overseas literature festivals to represent "our people". Writers and satirists personally targeted by Erdoğan, in contrast, were branded "traitors" when they gave speeches abroad and were put in their place. A new law was devised concerning the translation subsidy given to writers whose books were to be published abroad, so only writers favoured by the administration were "selected with the meticulousness of a surgeon". Ultimately, "our people"'s meatballs have ended up strangling Macbeth to death, and "our people" were encouraged to boo him at his funeral.

Now, all the artists, actors, intellectuals, writers and journalists who live in Cihangir discuss these issues. After a while, they start laughing from their fury. There isn't much to move their souls except for the tiny private theatre companies and the small satirical magazines that keep popping up daily ... Some of us, however, pay a heavier price for Erdoğan's targeting of all those who are not conservative, Sunni, male and like him, through the repeated use of "these people". This incident takes place on the night of 18 February 2015 in Kadıkoy ...

A journalist friend, Nuh Köklü, had lost his job after the Gezi protests, like dozens of other journalists. He had to suffer the same fate as all those who wanted to be unbiased news reporters. Nuh was an active member of one of the neighbourhood solidarity committees that started after the Gezi protests. He would buy pet food from a grocery store near the place where the committee meetings were held and leave it on the street so that stray animals wouldn't die of hunger on cold, snowy winter nights. Forty-six-year-old Nuh was long-haired, a socialist, he had not "chosen poverty", as the TV channel he had been fired from said he had when it broadcast news of his death. He was just a journalist who had been deprived of a job. As he was returning home late one night on an evening when he, along with his girlfriend and friends, had protested against the Internal Security Law, which would give incomprehensible authority to the police, they started to have a snowball fight. One of the snowballs hit the display window of the grocery store where he bought pet food. The grocer came out and stabbed Nuh Köklü to death. The punishment of "these people" had been a long time coming! Nuh's last words seared the hearts of all who knew him and knew what a decent person he was:

"Please let this be a dream!"

AKP's most derided party slogan in recent years was: "It was a dream but it came true". Yes, someone stabbing a journalist who was having a snowball fight because a snowball hit his window could only have been a nightmare, but now it had really come true. The people openly declared that they would stop at nothing to punish "these people". Quite understandably anxious that "hate killings" would grow more frequent, the thousands of people who walked behind the coffin at the funeral of Nuh Köklü were well aware that the same thing could happen to them some day.

The snowman – sorry, snow*woman* – incident that took place about a month later unsurprisingly also failed to be amusing. Students who built a snowwoman instead of a snowman in the schoolyard had called over their teacher so they could all pose for a photograph. An investigation was filed against the female teacher for "acting out of accordance with the values of society". The hegemony cloaking the country couldn't even abide snowmen and snowwomen that weren't monotypic. The olives that stood in for nipples on the snowwoman could irrevocably deprave the morals of society! "These people" ought to be apprehended where they stood!

Night is descending. Shall we walk to Taksim, the heart of Istanbul? And wrap up this long day? But what are those kids over there doing? Dark children running through the throngs of Arab tourists from Gulf countries and flashing the peace sign at the tourists hailing from Western countries … what victory could these poor shoe-shining kids have won? Why do the poorest and darkest kids of a country make the peace sign? And why, when they spy the police, do they hastily hide their peace-signing fingers and run away?

OPPOSITE MEANINGS OF THE PEACE SIGN: KURDS AND TURKS

On 16 November 2014, gleeful adults and children all over the world tweeted selfies of themselves making the peace sign. To support and give morale to the Kurdish guerrilla organisation

YPG, Twitter user @JessicaGG25 had started the tag #ShowYourV4YPG and asked her supporters to spread it. With the appeal "Pls join and/or RT campaign supporting brave YPG vs ISIS", the campaign started by @JessicaGG25 took Twitter by storm. The militant women of YPG were already at their most beautiful, bravest and most assured about victory, not only on Twitter but in the international press as well. So much so that they had even participated in a shoot for the French *Marie Claire*. During these days when the peace sign and the militant men and women of YPG were so endearing and acceptable in the eyes of the world, something entirely different took place in Erzurum. The women's football team of Diyarbakır, considered to be the putative capital of the Kurdish region, played against Samsun in the notoriously right-wing and nationalist city of Erzurum, winning epically with a score of 24–0. The Kurdish footballers were subjected to a disciplinary investigation for making the peace sign while running around the pitch at the end of the game in celebration of their crushing victory. Around the same time, news circulated that a woman who had flashed the peace sign during the Prime Minister's rally in Ağrı, once again a Kurdish province, had been pulled into the AKP party building and beaten. Right afterwards in the city of Batman, in what is once again a Kurdish province, a woman who made the peace sign at President Erdoğan's bus during one of his rallies was taken into custody. The sign of the Kurdish guerrillas fighting against the relentless ISIS at Turkey's Syrian border, the last frontier of the Western world, might have been endearing and acceptable west of Istanbul, but inside Turkey's border areas it still represented a specific camp in another war. Even the little kids who flash the peace sign at the police in Taksim Square instinctively know that the story of this sign is also the history of the Kurdish people.

For the rest of the world, the mention of the peace sign might bring Winston Churchill to mind. On this soil, however, when you mention the peace sign, "It's the sign of the Kurds," Turkish nationalists will scowl and Kurds will smile. "The sign of the PKK," to be more accurate. This piece of information goes back to the 1980s. Turkey frequently saw this pose struck by Kurdish militants on TV and in newspapers: right hand raised, making the peace sign; left hand over the face to avoid recognition. This was seen so often that I remember that whenever young people took a group photo in the 1990s, they would teasingly strike this pose. The sarcastic posturing was often accompanied by the phrase that militants caught in the 1980s used to say:

"Our activities shall continue!"

As someone who spent her adolescence in the west of Turkey in the 1990s, let me tell you: it was a societal disease that we were able to joke about, we were so insensitive to the fate of these young people whom we more or less comprehended were about to be thrown in jail and tortured. We were a people made diseased. For as people who were children in the 1980s and growing up during the 1990s, every evening when we sat down to dinner, we would see news broadcasts from south-eastern Turkey showing the bodies of the Kurdish militants caught in the mountains. In newscaster speak, we would be informed that "terrorists apprehended in their caves were captured dead" and we would go on eating. These people never had faces and there was no other news concerning the region. There were only those faceless people who wandered around up in the mountains and "attacked our country". This was only one method of dehumanising the enemy. We didn't even have to stop to wonder at length who these dehumanised people were, why they were killed, or why they were wandering around up in the mountains in the first place. I remember that one night after such a news broadcast, my father, who had taught at a primary school in the Kurdish region when he was young, told the following story from the 1960s at the dinner table:

"When I first went there, I saw that the kids didn't speak Turkish. We weren't told. No one told us that the people there were Kurds, that they spoke Kurdish. I wrote to the capital and asked for book recommendations for teaching Turkish to the kids. In turn they called me to the capital. 'You were deceived, there are no people called Kurds, Kurdish does not exist,' they said to me."

My father said that after this incident he had to give up teaching and, growing rueful, tried to teach us some of the meagre Kurdish he had learned there. It took years for me to realise that this minor, indistinct childhood memory was actually the origin of the story of the people who were dying on TV. I would hazard a guess that in many homes in the west of Turkey, such stories were being told, even if only in hushed tones. Many knew, one way or another, why the Kurds rebelled, why they were dehumanised by the state, why these people were being killed; but they chose to stay silent in the face of the "common enemy of the nation". Or to speak in a low voice …

"This state has beat into us the knowledge that we are Kurdish."

Years later, after I had learned well enough what the Kurdish problem was, Dr Mahmut Ortakaya and I were having a chat in a small coffee house in Diyarbakır when he told me this in the strange, poignant yet joyful Kurdish lilt of his elderly voice. The socialist doctor and founder of the Helsinki Citizens' Assembly has witnessed first-hand the recent political history of the Kurds. He, among others, told me about the cogs in the centre of the Kurdish heart, which I knew a little about now, on a visit to Diyarbakır. They said things like this ...

Cruelty does not cause rebellion. A man's patience is bigger than himself. But cruelty makes one lose one's humanity. As one witnesses one's wretchedness, one collects shame. That person is unable to withstand not the cruelty but the shame. Rebellion begins when all the paths leading away from shame have been exhausted, not before. The crowds worship not leaders but the intolerableness of the shame. Workers, the impoverished, the people and occupied nations all rise up to stave off shame.

When the oppressed rise up, the first thing they learn is that they must be as harsh as the oppressor. To give meaning to their struggle, they will write their own poems and legends. People are stirred by words. Legends, heroes, myths and cults accumulate over time. Resistance becomes a space of life. Those left out are now part of the shame, not of the people. The wheels turn. Their circulation speeds up as authority diabolises any resistance. A child born in Diyarbakır has little choice now over whether or not he wants to be a "guerrilla" ...

It's too late to tell what has happened. It's always too late to tell the original old story that caused the mobilisation. The story of a Kurd begins at the point she is silent. Telling her sorrowful story, she stops at a certain point and says, "Never mind ..." She thinks you can't handle the rest. It's a Middle Eastern tradition to try to laugh while relaying the most deplorable things, to try to make you laugh. For if one "falls apart" one can never be put back together. So many bloody stories in Diyarbakır are told amidst jokes. They don't tell one another these stories, since everyone has been through the same thing. And since usually no one from elsewhere asks about the past ... well, the story is never really told.

The following is what comes after the "anyway" part of the story. Why is it that when, allegedly, PKK leader Abdullah Öcalan's hair was forcibly cut in prison, children as young as twelve went out into the streets to demonstrate and then had to serve twenty years' imprisonment? Why is it that young men vanish and go up into the mountains as soon as, or even before, they finish high school? Why do these people spill out into the squares every Nowruz, the celebration that marks the beginning of spring? Why are car tyres set on fire in the ghettos of our cities? Why does the voice of a Kurdish businessman so "assimilated" that he owns skyscrapers shake when he talks about childhood experiences? Finally, why do Kurdish members of Parliament have to serve life in prison for swearing in in Kurdish at the parliamentary podium? The people we will talk about now represent the state of the wound before it turned into fury and mobilisation. They are the heart.

Of the millions of people who have seen a guerrilla on TV, very few know how Kurdish children grow up. How their childhood wounds lead either to complete muteness or to screaming. Could one who is not Kurdish understand it at all? What I am about to tell you is a foray into the long answer to that question.

Diyarbakır … six young lawyers laugh. The subject at hand is their primary school memories. The switch made from a "fresh almond branch" that they were beaten with for three years for not being able to say "bathroom" in Turkish … the blows from a ruler on the tips of their joined fingers for every Kurdish word that escaped from their lips in a classroom where Kurdish was forbidden … the spying children were instructed to do on their parents to prevent Kurdish from being spoken at home … "How we even ended up with proper jobs," says Mahsuni. "Sometimes it amazes me."

"No one knows in the west of Turkey," I say. "Tell me, how does a Kurdish child grow up?" Ahmet grows angry:

"After all that I've been through. That my parents and my siblings have gone through … I have to talk about it now too, do I? Is there anything more humiliating than that? You have to go and prove your suffering, too."

* * *

The young lawyers talk about being "stuck" between the two powers of the region. Their beloved teachers who were killed by the PKK, then the beating they received from the Turkish Armed Forces to make them "talk" about the circumstances of the deaths of those same teachers. Whenever a voice sinks, another feels compelled to say something they can laugh (!) about:

"Once they got hung up on the dogs. 'According to our intelligence, the dogs don't bark at the guerrillas, they bark at the soldiers.' There goes the whole village to receive a beating!"

Another funny (!) story: "I was heading into the village on a bus. The soldiers stopped us. The old man next to me whipped out his ID. I got angry with him for taking out his ID without being asked. 'My dear son,' he says to me, 'Do you know the story of the old ox? They take the old ox out to the market. Everyone is looking at his teeth. Finally the ox began to grin whenever he saw someone coming. That's what they've turned us into!' What can I say? In between the weapons of a silent old generation and the younger one ..."

Amidst their laughter, the stories they had forgotten as a survival mechanism conjure up others: "Remember Feyzo? They were putting the whole village through a walloping again. It was Feyzo's turn. The soldier asks, 'Feyzo, is that you?' Feyzo hollers, 'May God forbid it, commander!'" In the midst of the laughter comes an icy sentence: "In the end you become too afraid to even say, 'It's me,' you know? Never mind ..."

* * *

The most difficult thing to comprehend about the Kurds for someone in the west is their unique loyalty to Abdullah "Apo" Öcalan. In fact, the same people who can laugh over bloody stories don't have a single joke involving him. He is sacrosanct, in a way. Why?

Nebahat Akkoç, who established the Women's Centre in Diyarbakır and was listed among *The Times*' 100 heroes of the year a few years back, is a figure prominent in both the

Kurdish and women's movements. Frequently critical of the PKK, Nebahat tells me: "There was a girl from Sason named Dilan. Both the organisation and Öcalan were being criticised at a meeting. She jumps to her feet and starts yelling. 'I won't let you speak ill of Öcalan. No one took us seriously until he showed up.' They were led to believe that they were being taken seriously thanks to him." Because he was accepted as the symbol of unity and resistance instead of scattered submission, because becoming scattered again would mean annihilation …

I ask the lawyers what they think of Abdullah Öcalan, or, in their words, the "leadership":

"You have to ask us all that privately, somewhere else." They are reticent around one another when it comes to talking about Apo. It isn't easy. Respect? Fear? They simper. "Never mind," they say, "let's not get into that." I ask the same question to one of the most esteemed figures in Kurdish politics, who wishes to remain anonymous. He explains: "Without Apo, there would be ten PKKs, not one. The Kurdish people would open fire on one another and on Turkey. His presence is crucial to Kurds staying united no matter what."

* * *

In Diyarbakır, the septuagenarian MD Mahmut Ortakaya laughed as he opened the passenger door for me to get into his car:

"Since motorised transport around here started with pickups, and in the back you have peers and animals, with Kurds the passenger seat is still the convention. Hop in."

Dr Ortakaya has a political history ranging from founding the Workers' Party of Turkey to membership of the Helsinki Citizens' Assembly. Everything that happened to this land happened to him as well. He should be referred to as a physician who rises above history to look at events with the coolness of universal values, a Kurdish luminary. He has the "sorrowful eloquence" of someone who was fortified by the grief of having to tell soldiers in the 1990s who were force-feeding Yeşilyurt villagers their own faeces, "If you make these people eat faeces, how will we teach them to wash their hands after going to the toilet?" He also knows that the unknowns about Kurds aren't limited to subtleties of convention: "The most important thing Turks don't know are the trials of the Kurds during their adventure of Turkification."

He laughs again: "You don't even want to eat a cucumber with GMOs. Then why mess with the genetics of the Kurds?"

With all the mirth it's hard, but finally we go back to his story, and the 1940s.

"My friend tickled me as the Turkish national anthem was playing. The teachers had whips made of sheep's intestines. Got such a walloping! Listen, let me tell you something: back then I didn't know I was a Kurd. *They* knew we were Kurds. Only now I understand that they knew. And in time they beat into us that we were Kurds."

"We have no right to make children racist," says Mahmut Ortakaya, "and you cannot pour children into the mould of 'I am a Kurd, I am honest, I am hardworking'." He is referring to the oath that primary school children in Turkey recite every morning. The oath starts:

"I am a Turk, I am honest, I am hardworking ..."

And ends:

"My existence shall be dedicated to the Turkish existence."

Dr Ortakaya tells me about how his own childhood was poured into a mould:

"After the revolution of 1960, they made a list. 'This village has this many guns, if we don't get those guns ...' When they didn't, they stripped the village's men naked and shut them up someplace. Then they brought the women. When they suddenly let the men loose ... They made us actors in so many such plays. Like Seyit Rıza said at the Dersim Massacre, 'This is a shame, it is a sin, it is cruelty.' But still, you should write it as ... never mind." So, what comes after "never mind"?

"Turks are the Kurds' best friends. But a friendship should be based on honour."

A sad pause.

"Conscience, mercy ... these are the traits of humanity. You don't have to have an education. A human being would understand, if he knew what was endured ... a human being would understand."

Let's leave Diyarbakır and return to Istanbul ...

A Kurd at the top of one of Istanbul's skyscrapers, not a single worry. Cigar in one hand, payroll in the other. What worries could he have?

"You keep your mouth shut," he says. "Just when you're talking big money with the guys at the top, there's the news on TV. One of the men curses Kurds to Hell and you keep your mouth shut. To avoid unpleasantness. Or ... never mind."

"You become too afraid to say it's me," that is. Whether you're a skinny seven-year-old in the village or a seventy-year-old hotshot at the top of a skyscraper.

"It's odd," says Nebahat Akkoç, in Diyarbakır:

"We all learned Turkish by having it beaten into us. Now we do our literature and politics in this language. Who knows, maybe we'll never understand our own wounds."

Nebahat Akkoç's husband, a teacher, was put in the Diyarbakır Prison in the 1980s and became the victim of an unresolved murder in 1993. She brought up her two children on her own, was taken into custody dozens of times, and tortured. That is to say, she led the "normal" life of anyone in the Kurdish region who stands at an equal distance from the PKK and the state.

"What is the most disappointing thing, for you, that Turks don't know?," I ask her.

"What was before the PKK. They think it all started with the PKK," she replies. "Although actually …"

And so we go back to Nebahat's childhood, to the 1960s.

The city of Silvan. Nebahat is small. Soldiers conduct a search. Taking her short-haired sister for a boy, they ransack her home. As they leave, Nebahat chases after them with the other kids. They hide somewhere from where they can see the village square. They've rounded up all the men in the village, dragging them over the ground, then beating them. "A Kurdish child has witnessed this dozens of times by the time she's grown," says Nebahat "Her father beaten, her mother cursed at. This has nothing to do with the PKK.

That's where the fury lies." She says the same thing: "I'm in awe of my children. How they managed to grow up, how they have regular jobs and lives."

Why?

It's the 1990s. Her kids are preparing for the university exams, studying through the night. Nebahat buys the heaviest black curtain fabric she can find. So the police won't see the lights, will think no one's home and leave. For she has applied to the European Court of Human Rights about her husband's unsolved murder and is constantly being detained and tortured …

"Torture every time. So that the kids wouldn't see the state I'm in, every time I come back home … never mind …"

The Kurds never had the chance to tell what came after the "never mind", nor did Turks ever want to hear it. And so a roughly thirty-five-year-long war grew, intensified and spread from 1980 to 2016.

This was only a fraction of the Kurds' recollections, but what of the recollections of the state, and thus Turkey's west, of the Turks? That was a different history entirely. The two completely disparate histories written on the same soil is the very reason the war continues to be waged … The peace sign triggered two different histories in the minds of the people who saw it. For Kurds, the sign meant hope; for pro-establishment Turks, hate. Let's take a look at the history of the "establishment" behind the peace sign in order to understand why the war continues.

OFFICIAL MEMORY VERSUS
ACTUAL MEMORY

[In the era of the Ottoman Empire, the end of the 1800s] the "national awakening" and rebellions that started in Macedonia leapt to the East, giving rise to a large number of uprisings in the region. The first awakening in the East found its locus with the Armenians. Though not as widespread as the Armenians, a serious ideal of national awakening amongst Kurdish and Arab intellectuals also arose in this period.

Thinking precaution necessary due to local predicaments in the East, Sultan Abdul Hamid hoped to bring Kurdish *Bey*s, landlords, closer to the state by awarding them some special distinctions and concessions. As necessitated by this policy, the Sultan took children of Kurdish *Bey*s into the palace to provide them with an education, honouring the tribe leaders through direct contact and the development of personal friendships. Thanks to the direct relationships he established, the Sultan was able to renew the Kurds' trust and keep Eastern borders under control. More importantly, the Pan-Islamist policy that Sultan Abdul Hamid undertook in the face of Western imperialism found enormous support amongst the Kurds. In this period, the Sultan founded the Hamidiye Corps [comprised of Kurdish fighters and used during the great exile of the Armenians] in order to suppress a potential Armenian rebellion. In addition, he opened schools under the name of Imperial Tribal Schools where education was given in Kurdish as a way of keeping matters under his control. Thanks to his politics, Sultan Abdul Hamid gained the trust of the Kurds and received the title *"Bave Kürdan"* meaning "Father of the Kurds". (Political scientist Hüseyin Yayman, *Turkey's Memory of the Kurdish Problem*, 2011)

If anyone is wondering why we had to go back to the late 1800s to understand the peace sign children in Taksim flash at the police before running away, let me explain.

The Turkish state's and political authority's outlook on the Kurdish problem is nearly the same in the 2000s as it was in the late 1800s!

According to political scientist Hüseyin Yayman, who during his research into the state's memory concerning the Kurdish issue has compiled in a book the near forty reports on the Kurdish problem produced since the founding of the Republic, Turkey's Kurdish politics are roughly divided into five parts:

"The first is the 1918–25 period when the independence struggle took place and the existence of the Kurds was accepted. The second is the 'denial and assimilation' period between 1925 and 1960, during which the state developed its official arguments. The third, starting with the right-wing Democrat Party administration and extending into the 1970s, is the period of 'expectation'. The fourth, between 1970 and 1980, is the period of 'awareness'. The fifth and last is the period that began with the advent of the PKK."

Reading all forty or so reports gives one a sense of the following. Those state officials who learn about the situation by travelling to the Kurdish region either suggest resolving the problem in a completely fascist, assimilatory approach and with militaristic methods, or agree with the Kurds even if they barely admit it, demanding fair treatment by the state of the region's citizens. Reports of the second type are always ignored whereas reports that advocate pressure are immediately acknowledged.

The one reality that all of these reports recognise one way or another is the state of imposed economic and social underdevelopment in the region.

It's important to note that the Kurdish region, which encompasses east and south-eastern Anatolia, officially lived under conditions of martial law from 1978 up until 2002 and has continued to live an extraordinary life ever since. We are talking about a region that, although it has existed under wartime conditions since the late 1970s, is never acknowledged by the state as being actively at war. The phrase the state came up with to describe it was the same for decades: high-intensity conflict. Those who called the state of affairs a war were readily accepted to be representatives of "the enemy".

A tragicomic detail: although in Turkish consonants are pronounced with an -eh at the end, saying "peh-keh-keh" could put you in the position of being a representative of the enemy. You should call it "pay-ka-ka" instead, pronounced the way the state has fabricated it.

Since the founding of the Republic, there have been two dominant points of view on the Kurdish region:

1. There is no such thing as Kurds or Kurdish. "Kurd" is an onomatopoeia that was derived from the crunching sound one makes while walking about in the snow on the mountains. Kurds are really Turks.
2. Kurds exist, but their only problem is their economy and lack of education.

Each containing varying amounts of violence, the two assimilatory points of view have led administrations to produce policies just like those of Sultan Abdul Hamid's: bargaining with the land barons of the region.

Because the "land reform" suggested by the leftist movement and left-wing parties throughout the 1970s was rejected every time, the state was able to "solve" the Kurdish problem only by reaching out to the feudal *bey*s. Minus the freedom of Kurdish education granted by Abdul Hamid, of course. The state's cooperation with feudal lords continued until the mid-1980s. The nightmare that changed it all was Diyarbakır Prison. With the 1980 military coup, yes, all prisons were turned into enormous torture chambers. But anyone who has lived through those times knows and acknowledges that what the Kurds suffered in Diyarbakır was like nothing seen before or since. The unspeakable tortures inflicted during that period are currently the focus of oral history research that is difficult to peruse. I cannot give this list here, because I cannot find it in myself as a human being to write the words. Zülfikar Tak, who himself had been held at the Diyarbakır Prison, rendered in pencil the humanly incomprehensible tortures inflicted by soldiers brandishing truncheons reading, "Allah is not in, the prophet is on vacation!" I suggest that you type his name into Google and see what comes up. For I feel like merely writing down these tortures would tarnish one's soul.

It was when four prisoners set themselves on fire in protest at the torture in Diyarbakır Prison that the fire of a rebellion was kindled as well. The PKK was born of the limitless cruelties of Diyarbakır Prison. Delivering their first attack in 1984, the organisation became the most useful enemy of first the fascist junta and then the civilian administrations that succeeded it throughout the 1980s and 1990s. The most striking aspects of the Kurdish problem that made a mark on the 1990s were the unsolved murders known to have been committed by the illegal apparatus of the state. Journalists, businessmen, politicians, intellectuals and writers were killed or went missing. The tortures inflicted in Diyarbakır Prison in the 1980s and the dark days of the 1990s only started to be talked about in the 2000s, yet due to the ongoing war neither the tortures nor the murders were perceived as a national disgrace. Many thought the declarations to be "fabricated by the terrorists". The oral history research was limited to leftist circles. Mothers who lost their children to unsolved murders, and their search for and discovery of their children's bones, were never respected. The operation of blunting suffering was such a success that even the suffering of a Kurdish mother who wore around her neck the bones of her child that she had found at long last could be considered "propaganda for an illegal organisation".

The more the existence of the Kurds was denied, the more widely and severely human rights were breached in the region, and the more the PKK grew and strengthened throughout the

1980s and 1990s. The organisation begat not only armed militants but also university students practising civilian politics. It took part in every civilian organisation and, more importantly, succeeded in creating public opinion in Europe and getting in touch with international bodies. As a result of this expansion and reinforcement, feudal lords were no longer the Kurds' only means to political power. The armed organisation was also a movement of modernisation for the region. It was the PKK that brought a left-wing vision to a region notorious for its religious reactionism. Although its left-wing front was left in the shadow of nationalist demands after the 1990s, the organisation broke the hegemony of the religious and feudal lords in the region with whom the state had familiarised itself. Although property relationships weren't changed entirely, the moral and political power and the state's armed aggressor in the region were now the PKK. In a way, just as fascism in Turkey gained depth of meaning with the phrase "Every Turk is born a soldier", so an increasingly higher number of Kurds in the region were born guerrillas.

The late 1990s and early 2000s went by with Kurdish politicians and intellectuals struggling to explain themselves to Western intellectuals. As someone who attended most of these meetings, I would like to note an interesting detail. For I feel that it reflects the racism that is instilled in even the most sensitive, educated and open-minded people of Turkey. Some of these meetings were held in Istanbul but then often followed up with meetings in Kurdish provinces. Most of the intellectuals and journalists who attended the meetings in Diyarbakır or in other Kurdish provinces dressed like they were going on a safari. Women who usually wore heels and skirts were in trainers and khakis; men similarly wore more casual get-ups rather than suits. The Kurdish participants who received us, on the other hand, would be dressed much more formally. I can't have been the only one irritated by this demeanour of "we are going into the war zone now", or "we are going to the underdeveloped rural area". The prerequisite equality wasn't something that came easily even to those who desired it.

In terms of the Kurdish issue, the 2000s were most significantly marked by AKP's "initiative policy". AKP's method was exactly that of the politics of Abdul Hamid. Let us emancipate Kurdish education and publishing, implement a pan-Islamist policy, and thus form an alliance with our "Kurdish brothers", in the words of Tayyip Erdoğan. The state TV channel began broadcasting in Kurdish for the first time. Naturally, an administration that employed Sultan Abdul Hamid's policies generally broadcast religious programmes on this channel. And also naturally, the intellectuals picked by AKP to legitimise its initiative policy were figures approved by the powers that be. Figures who criticised the administration were hence not invited to these "initiative meetings". The policy dubbed the "Kurdish initiative" in the press was immediately corrected by AKP for fear of a nationalist backlash:

"National unity and brotherhood project!"

The initiative policy, presented as a democratisation project in AKP's first term in power, changed direction in 2007 when AKP assumed power for its second term. Now Erdoğan was saying:

"According to these results, the most powerful representative for the Kurds in Turkey is AKP. We are the real representatives of the Kurds of Turkey; the results of this election make this evident. Our citizens of Kurdish origin have preferred AKP above any other party."

Despite the "peace negotiations" that the state has continued to hold from 2007 onwards with PKK leader Abdullah Öcalan, who was and is still being detained at Imralı Prison, President Recep Tayyip Erdoğan arrived at a point where he claimed: "There is no Kurdish problem. It's some Kurdish citizens who have problems." The inconsistency on the level of political power also made its way into the press, to the intelligentsia. That's why, if you ask me today, "Is it still taboo to talk about the Kurdish problem in Turkey?", I can only answer:

"It depends on Mr Erdoğan's mood today!"

* * *

For decades, as the Kurds wrote their own history in the east of the country, the government in the west taught us another history. It's a great challenge today for two peoples to make peace in the total sense of the word as the multiplying layers of memory estrange them more and more. If you were to talk of "living as brothers" in the east today, some would answer, as they well should, "We don't want to be brothers; we want to be friends." What the country really needs, if you ask me, is not a Kurdish initiative but a "Turkish initiative". All the families of Turkey who have faithfully kept on sending soldiers into a thirty-five-year war partially – and rightfully – protest about this sudden change in policy. They ask, "Then why did our sons fight? Why did they die?" The political authorities cannot give an answer for the prompt debasement of the concept of "martyrdom in the struggle against the PKK", a concept that has been sanctioned for thirty-five years. They cannot say, "Sorry! We sent your sons off to their deaths as part of a purposeless and cruel policy of oppression!"

I feel like we've talked enough about the Kurds today. If you ask me, the Kurdish people deserve to be in Turkey's future chapter much more than its present.

TOMORROW

"WHAT WILL BECOME OF THIS BRIDGE OF OURS?"

"How long is tomorrow? Eternity and a day." – ***Eternity and a Day***, film directed by Theo Angelopoulos

"Well, what makes a homeland then? What is it that you miss?"

I asked this question on a night in Tunisia in the summer of 2010 as radical Islamists surrounded Carthage, brandishing torches, shouting "Allahu Akbar" and threatening to burn down this neighbourhood where rich seculars lived. At the time, I was staying there to work on my novel. Because:

1. I had been fired from my job with a phone call that lasted 1.2 minutes:

   "Ece, you know why."

   "Yes."

   "Sorry."

   "Thank you."

   Too short to be tragic!

2. The social media trolls of the party in power, who received allowances – although this was not yet known – started an attack against me from thousands of accounts under various identities (AKP supporter, liberal, Kurd, socialist, anything you looked for you could find). Banding together, they created a new identity for me:

   An ignorant, dumb, spoilt, pitiful, malevolent woman playing the victim! It seemed everybody hated me.

There were so many of them that I came to believe the entire country thought of me this way. Others did too. I might quite possibly be among the first in my country to find out – all on my own at that – how easy it is "virtually" to create an ugly and false reality about a person. I remember the day months later when I finally pulled myself together and tweeted that defaming social figures is a weapon of psychological warfare: "Oh wow! So you do take yourself that seriously. You poor paranoid thing!" The ridicule was so awful that I had started sympathising with the death and rape threats I was receiving at the time.

So why does one long for a country where she assumes everyone hates her? That's the only question left in my mind from those days. The question of "What is a homeland?" that I asked while I was threatened both by phantoms from my country out for blood and by shadows in a foreign country brandishing torches:

"What is the homeland that you continue to long for now, right this minute?"

In those days, I had described the homeland as Angelopoulos had described the concept of tomorrow in his masterpiece. I still do.

The homeland is actually a table! The homeland is a table around which you sit with your loved ones, all of you laughing together, and the eternal void that surrounds it. The homeland is as concrete and finite as the instant you laugh with your loved ones and as abstract and infinite as the void that surrounds it.

After that evening, the homeland became something else for me, changing the meaning of the piece of land and concept

272

I had been thinking about and writing newspaper articles on for twenty years. You eventually stop being angry or resentful at a lover who has hurt you deeply; you can no longer shout. A deep place of silence hollows out inside you, dark and locked up. This is the kind of place hollowed out inside me with regard to my homeland. Since I was afraid that if I lifted up the scab the bleeding would never stop, I never picked at it; I never wrote about my homeland. It was like not using an injured limb so you wouldn't have to feel the pain. I still don't use it. That's why I have withdrawn from daily reality and sought refuge in the truth of literature. It is from the shore of that truth that I have attempted to write this book.

The reason I mention this overly personal matter is this.

You will be reading about "tomorrow", the loveliest word in all languages, in sentences formed by one such damaged psyche. But this damaged writer is someone who knows that it would be enormously arrogant – and equally ignorant – to think that the truth is limited to her own reality. I hope I can write without doing injustice to my homeland and myself.

The question of what will become of Turkey naturally prompts answers with personal consequences. It doesn't only have judicial and political consequences on a national level, the answers to the questions "What kind of person will I be?" and "What kind of life will I lead?" also concern the country's future. During my career as a journalist, I met many people from many countries who chose to or were forced to leave their countries, were deserted by their countries, or were left without countries. For those who had enough words to tell their stories, verbally or in writing, there weren't many options for existing. Some of these people translated their disappointment in their homeland and the grief of their losses into fury and based their existence on their resentment against those who ruled their country. Their resentment against the homeland became their reason for existing. This type of resentment and the rhetoric or literature of victimhood have an international web of customers, and those who live by this rhetoric can spend their whole lives saying the same things to their audience over and over again.

I witnessed those too proud to express their fury become completely mute. They drifted around like the ghosts of the earth. A concept ought to be invented in international law to describe their melancholy so that their level of dejection can be compensated for. But it doesn't exist.

Ultimately, as difficult as it is to love one's homeland without shame or pride, it is just as difficult to describe one's suffering because of it on foreign soil without fury or an absurd zest.

I describe my homeland – thank God – still as an insider, still from within. That's why the readers of this book won't just be "foreigners" who know little about the homeland but also the "shadows" that live within it. That's rather scary. Because there is a considerable distance between what you will tell a foreigner about your country and what you will tell a fellow citizen, no matter how much you try to close the gap. The more the writer considers that gap, the more she feels like she is betraying the truth, if not the homeland.

I chose to write this book as though I were talking to neither a foreigner nor a fellow citizen but to a good friend who is far away. This book envisions a reader willing to listen to the long, melancholy, entertaining and complicated answer to the question "Where are you from?" I, in turn, envision burdening the reader with a challenge. A challenge to expand the heart. I envision you, the next time you visit Istanbul, Cappadocia or Antalya, walking around not with the light step of the tourist but with the heaviness of heart of the millions asking, "What will become of this land of ours?" This tribulation, this heaviness, is a "landmark" that does not appear in the guidebooks, a "parameter" that isn't even mentioned in political analyses. This is the only way you will be able to understand why people in Turkey always attempt to understand the country's future with a stereotypical question: "What will become of this land of ours?"

Now let us answer the question that people ask with melancholy, and with laughter when they are tired of melancholy:

"What will become of this land of ours?"

* * *

For any political commentator it is very difficult to predict Turkey's future of politics unless you don't mind being mortified by your failed projections. After enjoying a tiny bit of hope with the 7 June 2015 elections, the Turkish and Kurdish opposition fell back into regression – this time worse than before the Gezi uprising. The outcome was a coalition but this simply did not please President Erdoğan, and therefore he pushed for the repetition of the election and eventually succeeded. President Erdoğan made his famous statement "Turkey will be unstable if it is not ruled by a single party". In between the first and the second election the country was a bloodbath due to the terror attacks. The single-party rule of AKP managed to remove the impunity of MPs which opened the way for the imprisonment of Kurdish MPs for being "terrorists". While this book was in preparation, Turkey was witnessing one of its most serious setbacks to democracy.

Since it is almost impossible to make any predictions for real politics, let us look beyond that, to a more inspiring picture.

APPETITE AND HOPE

"The psychological depth of literary characters: on the couch with the characters of the novel *Time of the Mute Swans*."

As you know, the longer the topic title, the fewer the number of listeners you are likely to get. That was why I had predicted the number of attendees at my talk about my latest novel at the Mersin University Psychology Club as thirty or forty. At most, with the addition of a merely curious bunch, fifty or sixty. When I went to the hall where the talk would be held, along with those crowded into the next room to watch the talk on the screens, there in front of me was a total of a thousand people.

The references in the questions that followed my brief talk ranged from Marx to Lacan and Foucault to Žižek. They were incredibly well informed, involved and spirited. My eyes filled with tears. Not because of the acclaim, but because I could only guess at the childhoods of the thousand young people sitting in front of me ...

Mersin University is in the south of Turkey; the city of Mersin is on the Mediterranean coast. It's the university preferred by

Kurdish youths from south-eastern and eastern Anatolia, the best they can hope to get into due to educational inequality. The young people sitting across from me were born in the late 1990s. Children growing up during the bloodiest times of civil war, mostly of provincial families forced to relocate to the cities in the mass migration brought on by the war.

They grew up in the shadow of bombs, fires, poverty, the harassment flights of warplanes and automatic weapons. They set out on life five steps behind in the godforsaken villages of godforsaken provinces. Nearly every one can identify the model of a warplane by its sound. It's almost a miracle that they are here as students rather than up in the mountains as guerrillas. Perhaps that's why they study, read and exist with guerrilla-like discipline. They are growing up as the children of a suppressed – and, more importantly, organised – people. Whereas their peers in the West have different opportunities for experience, they take life as seriously as only an organised individual can, as a matter of life and death. Let's take a short break.

DOWN! DOWN! DOWN! DOWN!

A few days before the 7 June 2015 elections in Diyarbakır, by all accounts the putative political capital of the Kurdish region, a bomb went off during a huge rally. Seen live from every corner of Turkey, the explosion provoked an unusual reaction from the crowd. Thousands of people sat down all at once. Nobody ran. Everyone just dropped down to the ground where they stood. Almost everyone was shouting in unison:

"Down! Down! Down! Down!"

It was a bizarre and at the same time tragic sight. For it revealed how accustomed everyone there was to war. They all knew that they could be fired upon from any one direction right after a bomb was detonated. They didn't need to think, didn't need directions or even a warning. Thousands of people were on the ground in seconds. After this attempt at provocation, Selahattin Demirtaş the leader of Kurdish party HDP, said: "We are an organised society." This wasn't news to those who knew the region and the Kurdish movement, but it jarred the rest of Turkey to see how familiar people were with war, with the lowest kind of war that targeted civilians. Yes, the Kurdish people are an organised society. Since the moment they are born they are organised, down to their fingertips.

In 1980s' Turkey, in the midst of the breakdown of all political organisations, the political organisation of the Kurds was born. As I mentioned previously, this organisation also spread to the cities of the West during the 1990s. The Kurds brought up an educated generation in addition to the one they gave up to the war. It's a generation that is in step with the world, which has had to explain its issues to the world, with the discipline of an organisation that is open to the world without forgetting where it came from. Selahattin Demirtaş is in fact one of the pioneers of this generation. Others like him will follow. These young people, the legacy of the generations who paid a price, are hopeful, devoted, eager, and now full of the zeal and assurance that comes with their ascent to the political stage.

I'm talking about a political movement that also has legitimacy and renown in terms of international dynamics. It's possible now to follow YPG militants fighting against ISIS, especially the Kurdish militant women, in the international press. Even the Turkish TV channels broadcast their news with the organisation's name rather than saying "terrorists" as they used to in the past. An ironic twist of fate: the "Kurdish terrorists" against whom we defended our borders now defend the borders of Turkey against ISIS.

In light of all this, my prediction is that the next decade in Turkey and its surroundings will be the decade of the Kurds. It will be so not only politically but also culturally. Whether any political party in power will be able to explain this situation to the Turkish mothers who gave their sons to a murky thirty-year war and how, that's another problem entirely. But it's evident from this vantage point that the Kurds will rise onto the world stage in ways they never have before. This will doubtless have a great effect on Turkey's fate. We'll all see together. Don't forget that this is the political power of an armed organisation that has fought against the second largest army of NATO for thirty years. Perhaps the possibility of coming to resemble one's enemy should also be noted here. It's too early, however, to say anything about all that.

WOMEN AND CHILDREN FIRST!

In the movies, when there's a fire or a ship is sinking, someone always shouts:

"Women and children first!"

In Turkey, this is apparently taken backwards. As though women and children should be the first to be thrown into the flames or left to drown. A dark decade awaits the women and children of Turkey. If you ask me, women will have to take new measures to defend their safety. We'll be seeing more of such non-governmental organisations. For just last year, twenty-eight women who were under government protection were murdered. Our government isn't really into protecting women. I predict that in the next ten years, women will come forth with more civilian organisations because they will be obliged to for self-preservation.

According to the June 2015 peace survey of the Global Peace Index, Turkey is the 135th country out of 165. That is, Turkey is quite unpeaceful not just for women but also for everyone else. The societal relations brought about by political polarisation, as well as the constant threat of ethnic tension, the eradication of the final remaining traces of a social state by the horrific inequality in income distribution, the clashes on the borders due to Syria, and the radical Islamist militants freely roaming within the borders of Turkey … these are the first causes that come to mind. But there is yet another thing that will influence the next decade: the mess that is the education system.

In the past thirty years, the last decade especially, the education system has been changed dozens of times. The education received in Turkey differs vastly not merely between generations but even between those just five years apart in age. This looks like it might completely eradicate the common social code, which is problematic enough as it is. Children grow up receiving completely different educations not within different social classes due to economic reasons, but also within the same classrooms due to political and religious reasons. The dramatic decline in the quality of education is a problem that will define the future all on its own. I'm guessing that the gradual elimination of science and philosophy classes from public schools will give us an entirely unrecognisable generation.

MIDDLE EASTERNISATION AND THE QUESTION "SHOULD WE GO?"

Throughout the past decade, people have been talking about leaving the country with increasing frequency. Although this seems to have changed somewhat with the Gezi protests, the Middle Easternisation of day-to-day life compels the educated middle and upper classes to consider leaving. By Middle Easternisation, I don't just mean suffering the consequences of the occupations of Syria and Iraq. Political and social life has become as unpredictable as it is in the Middle East. This bestows upon us all exceedingly tumultuous lives. A whole lot can befall you even when you're not doing anything – that's what being a Middle Easterner is like. Increasingly, we all find ourselves paralysed inside a tempest of commotion. That's why, I assume, you might be seeing middle- or upper middle-class Turkish migrants in European cities more often in the near future.

In the past decade, many an analyst originating from a left-wing secular tradition has said that Turkey as we know it (secular, parliamentary, social state, constitutional) will meet its demise with the rapid expansion of Islamic conservatism hand in hand with neoliberalism. Such observations stemmed from AKP's unopposed rulership and its social engineering of the masses. Today, this point of view has lost some of its influence. Both regional and national dynamics are changing rapidly. There's only one thing that remains the same: Turkey's geographic location and a safety valve that we cannot seem to locate.

THE "SAFETY VALVE" THAT CANNOT BE LOCATED

In the early 1990s, when I first started my career in journalism – at nineteen – I was interviewing one of the most experienced politicians in Turkey when I asked, presumably out of overexcitement:

"So what'll become of this country?"

The elderly politician laughed, his expression reminding me that I was young enough to be his granddaughter:

"Sweet young lady, this country has a safety valve that no one seems able to locate. This country will be fine. It will always pull together at the last minute!"

I've thought about this safety valve business often in recent days. Maybe something like this actually exists and we all secretly depend on it.

BROKEN BRIDGES, NEW BRIDGES

These days, despite heavy criticism and opposition, a third bridge is being built that will stretch across the Bosphorus to connect Asia and Europe. Ironic. While the ties between the East and the West become more frayed each day, and Turkey is on the verge of assuming the last border post duty of civilisation as defined by the West, the construction of the bridge crawls along at a painstaking pace. The bridges keep multiplying but that does nothing for the state of being "on a bridge".

This country that appeared as a bridge between the East and the West defined itself by the West at its formation. Although, under the rule of AKP, this definition may have turned indeterminately and fully towards the East, the bridge remains standing. Those on the bridge now face both ways. They wait for the world to turn and that eternal day called tomorrow to begin before they can describe their new direction. I think that, although they never speak it aloud, they depend on the fact that the safety valve is there, somewhere.

What can I say? Our story ends here. I hope I have been able to describe my beloved country to the reader of this book sufficiently well for her to be able to warmly chat with those who fret and ask "What will become of this country of ours?" at any table she might sit at, some day, in Turkey.

INDEX